John P. Jones

Money

A speech of John P. Jones

John P. Jones

Money
A speech of John P. Jones

ISBN/EAN: 9783744723169

Printed in Europe, USA, Canada, Australia, Japan

Cover: Foto ©Suzi / pixelio.de

More available books at **www.hansebooks.com**

MONEY.

"Gold is a wonderful clearer of the understanding; it dissipates every doubt and scruple in an instant, accommodates itself to the meanest capacities, silences the loud and clamorous and brings over the most obstinate and inflexible. Philip of Macedon refuted by it all the wisdom of Athens, confounded their statesmen, struck their orators dumb, and at length argued them out of their liberties."

—ADDISON.

SPEECH

OF

HON. JOHN P. JONES,

OF NEVADA,

ON THE FREE COINAGE OF SILVER;

IN THE

UNITED STATES SENATE,

MAY 12 AND 13, 1890.

WASHINGTON.
1890.

SPEECH

OF

HON. JOHN P. JONES,

OF NEVADA.

On the bill (S. 2350) authorizing the issue of Treasury notes on deposits of silver bullion.

Mr. JONES, of Nevada, said:

Mr. PRESIDENT: The question now about to be discussed by this body is in my judgment the most important that has attracted the attention of Congress or the country since the formation of the Constitution. It affects every interest, great and small, from the slightest concern of the individual to the largest and most comprehensive interest of the nation.

The measure under consideration was reported by me from the Committee on Finance. It is hardly necessary for me to say, however, that it does not fully reflect my individual views regarding the relation which silver should bear to the monetary circulation of the country or of the world. I am, at all times and in all places, a firm and unwavering advocate of the free and unlimited coinage of silver, not merely for the reason that silver is as ancient and honorable a money metal as gold, and equally well adapted for the money use, but for the further reason that, looking at the annual yield from the mines, the entire supply that can come to the mints will at no time be more than is needed to maintain at a steady level the prices of commodities among a constantly increasing population.

In view, however, of the great divergency of views prevailing on the subject, the length of time which it was believed might be consumed in the endeavor to secure that full and rightful measure of legislation to which the people are entitled, and the possibility that this session of Congress might terminate without affording the country some measure of substantial relief, I was willing, rather than have the country longer subjected to the baleful and benumbing influences set in motion by the demonetization act of 1873, to join with other members of the Finance Committee in reporting the bill now under consideration.

Under the circumstances I wish at the outset of the discussion to say that I hold myself free to vote for any amendment that may be offered that may tend to make the bill a more perfect measure of relief, and that may be more in consonance with my individual views.

THE CONDITION OF THE COUNTRY.

The condition of this country to-day, Mr. President, is well calculated to awaken the interest and arouse the attention of thinking men. It can be safely asserted that no period of the world's history can exhibit a people at once so numerous and homogeneous, living under one form of government, speaking a common language, enjoying the same degree of personal and political liberty, and sharing, in so equal a degree, the same civilization as the population of the

JONES

United States. Eminently practical.and ingenious, of indomitable will, untiring energy, and unfailing hope; favored by nature with a domain of imperial expanse, with soil and climate of unequaled variety and beneficence, with every natural condition that can conduce to individual prosperity and national glory, it might well be expected that among such a people industry, agriculture, commerce, art, and science would reach an extent and perfection of development surpassing anything ever known in the history of mankind.

In some respects this expectation would appear to have been well founded. For several years past our farmers have produced an annual average of 400,000,000 bushels of wheat. Our oat crop for 1888 was 700,000,000 bushels, our corn crop 2,000,000,000 bushels, our cotton crop 7,000,000 bales. In that year our coal mines yielded 170,000,000 tons of coal, our furnaces produced 6,500,000 tons of pig iron and 3,000,000 tons of steel. Our gold and silver mines add more than $100,000,000 a year to the world's stock of the precious metals. We print 16,000 newspapers and periodicals, have in operation 154,000 miles of railroad and 250,000 miles of telegraph. The value of our manufactured products at the date of the last census was $5,400,000,000. Our farm lands at the same time were estimated at $10,000,000,000, our cattle at $2,000,000,000, our railroads at $6,000,-000,000, our houses at $14,000,000,000. It is not too much to say that there has been an increase of fully 50 per cent. in those values since the taking of the census of 1880. Our national wealth to-day is reasonably estimated at over $60,000,000,000.

Figures and facts such as these in the history of a young nation bespeak the presence not merely of great natural opportunities, but of a people marvelously apt and forceful. From such results should be anticipated the highest attainable prosperity and happiness. Our population is alert, aspiring, and buoyant, not given to needless repining or aimless endeavor, but, with fixity of purpose, presses ever eagerly on, utilizing every conception of the brain to supplement and multiply the possibilities of the hand, and at every turn subordinating the subtle forces of nature to the best and wisest purposes of man. No equal number of persons on the globe better deserve success, or are better adapted for its enjoyment.

But instead of finding, as we should find, happiness and contentment broadcast throughout our great domain, there are heard from all directions, even in this Republic, resounding cries of distress and dissatisfaction. Every trade and occupation exhibits symptoms of uneasiness and distrust. The farmer, the artisan, the merchant,—all share in the general complaint that times are hard, that business is "dull." The farmer is in debt, and is not realizing, on the products of his labor, the wherewithal to meet either his deferred or his current obligations; the artisan, when at work, finds himself compelled to share his earnings with some relative or friend who is out of employment; the merchant who buys his goods on time finds little profit in sales, and difficulty in making his payments.

WHAT IS THE DIFFICULTY?

What can it be, Mr. President, that has thus brought to naught all the careful estimates and painstaking computations, not of thousands, nor of hundreds of thousands, but of millions, of keen, shrewd, and far-seeing men? Our people take an intelligent interest in their business; they look ahead; they endeavor, as far as possible, to estimate correctly their assets and liabilities, so that on the day of reckoning they may be found ready. Why this universal failure of all classes to compute correctly in advance their situation on the coming pay-day? What potent and sinister drug has been secretly introduced into the veins of commerce that has caused the blood to flow so sluggishly—that has narcotized the commercial and industrial world?

All have been looking for the cause, and many think they have discovered it. With some it is "over-production," with others either a "high tariff" or a "tariff not sufficiently high." Some think it due to trusts and combinations, others to improved methods of production, or because the crops are overabundant or not abundant enough. Some ascribe the difficulty to speculation; others, to "strikes." All sorts of insufficient and contradictory causes are assigned for the same general and universal complaint. However inadequate in themselves, they serve to emphasize the universal recognition of a difficulty whose cause without close inquiry is likely to elude detection. But the evil is of such magnitude, it is so widespread and pervasive, that, without a knowledge of its cause, all effort at mitigation of its effects can but add to the confusion and intensify the difficulty.

It behooves us, therefore, as we value the prosperity and happiness of our people, to set ourselves diligently to the inquiry: What is the cause of the unrest and discontent now universally prevailing?

ONE SYMPTOM COMMON TO ALL INDUSTRIES.

In surveying the question broadly, to discover whether there is anything that affects the situation in common from the standpoint of varying occupations, we find one, and only one, uniform and unfailing characteristic; the prices of all commodities and of all property, except in money centers, have fallen, and continue falling. Such a phenomenon as a constant and progressive fall in the general range of prices has always exercised so baleful an influence on the prosperity of mankind that it never fails to arrest attention.

History gives evidence of no more prolific source of human misery than a persistent and long continued fall in the general range of prices. But, although exercising so pernicious an influence, it is not itself a cause, but an effect.

When a fall of prices is found operating, not on one article or class of articles alone, but on the products of all industries; when found to be not confined to any one climate, country, or race of people, but to diffuse itself over the civilized world; when it is found not to be a characteristic of any one year, but to go on progressively for a series of years, it becomes manifest that it does not and can not arise from local, temporary or subordinate causes, but must have its genesis and development in some principle of universal application.

WHAT PRODUCES A GENERAL FALL OF PRICES?

What, then, is it that produces a general decline of prices in any country? It is produced by a shrinkage in the volume of money, relatively to population and business, which has never yet failed to cause an increase in the value of the money unit, and a consequent decrease in the price of the commodities for which such unit is exchanged. If the volume of money in circulation be made to bear a direct and steady ratio to population and business, prices will be maintained at a steady level, and, what is of supreme importance, money will be kept of unchanging value. With an advancing civilization, in which a large volume of business is conducted on a basis of credit extending over long periods, it is of the uttermost importance that money, which is the measure of all equities, should be kept unchanging in value through time.

JONES

6

EFFECT OF A REDUCTION IN THE MONEY-VOLUME.

A reduction in the volume of money relatively to population and business, or, (to state the proposition in another form) a volume which remains stationary while population and business are increasing, has the effect of increasing the value of each unit of money, by increasing its purchasing power.

It is only within a comparatively recent period that an increasing value in the money unit could produce such widespread disturbance of industy as it produces to-day. In the rude periods of society commerce was by barter; and even for thousands of years after the introduction of money, credit, where known at all, was extremely limited. Under such circumstances changes in the volume and in the value of money, while operating to the disadvantage of society as a whole, could not instantly or seriously affect any one individual. An increase of 25 per cent. in one year in the value of the money unit—a change which now, by reason of existing contracts and debts, would entail universal bankruptcy and ruin—would not be seriously felt by a community in which no such contracts or debts existed, in which payments were immediate or at short intervals, and each individual parted with his money almost as soon as he received it.

Such proportion of the annual increase in the value of the money unit as could attach to any one month, week, or day would be wholly insignificant, and as most transactions were closed on the spot, no appreciable loss could accrue to any individual. Such loss as did accrue was shared in and averaged among the whole community, making it the veriest trifle upon any individual. But how is it in our day?

THAT EFFECT INTENSIFIED AS CIVILIZATION ADVANCES.

The inventions of the past one hundred years have established a new order of the ages. The revolution of industry and commerce, effected by the adaptation of steam and other forces of nature to the uses of man, have given to civilization an impetus exceeding anything known in the former experience of mankind. Under the operation of the new system, the rapidity and intensity with which, within that period, civilization has developed, is due in great part to an economic feature unknown to ancient civilization and practically unknown even to civilized society until the present century. That feature is the time-contract, by which alone leading minds are enabled to project in advance enterprises of magnitude and moment. It is only through intelligent and far-seeing plans and projections that in a complex and minutely classified system of industry great bodies of men can be kept in uninterrupted employment.

We have 22,000,000 workmen in this country. In order that they may be kept uninterruptedly employed it is absolutely necessary that business contracts and obligations be made long in advance. Accordingly, we read almost daily of the inception of industrial undertakings requiring years to fulfill. It is not too much to say that the suspension for one season of the making of time-contracts would close the factories, furnaces, and machine shops of all civilized countries.

The natural concomitant of such a system of industry is the elaborate system of debt and credit which has grown up with it, and is indispensable to it. Any serious enhancement in the value of the unit of money between the time of making a contract or incurring a debt and the date of fulfillment or maturity always works hardship and frequently ruin to the contractor or debtor.

JONES

Three-fourths of the business enterprises of this country are conducted on borrowed capital. Three-fourths of the homes and farms
that stand in the name of the actual occupants have been bought
on time, and a very large proportion of them are mortgaged for the
payment of some part of the purchase-money.

Under the operation of a shrinkage in the volume of money this
enormous mass of borrowers, at the maturity of their respective debts,
though nominally paying no more than the amount borrowed, with
interest, are, in reality, in the amount of the principal alone, returning a percentage of value greater than they received—more than in
equity they contracted to pay and oftentimes more, in substance, than
they profited by the loan. To the man of business this percentage
in many cases constitutes the difference between success and failure.
Thus a shrinkage in the volume of money is the prolific source of
bankruptcy and ruin. It is the canker that, unperceived and unsus-
pected, is eating out the prosperity of our people. By reason of the
almost universal inattention to the nature and functions of money
this evil is permitted, unobserved, to work widespread ruin and disaster. So subtle is it in its operations that it eludes the vigilance
of the most acute. It baffles all foresight and calculation; it sets at
naught all industry, all energy, all enterprise.

CONTRAST OF EFFECTS PRODUCED BY AN INCREASING AND A DECREASING MONEY-VOLUME.

The difference in the effects produced by an increasing and a decreasing money-volume has not escaped the attention of observant
writers.

David Hume, in his Essay on Money, says:

It is certain that since the discovery of the mines in America industry has increased in all the nations of Europe. * * We find that in every kingdom into
which money begins to flow in greater abundance than formerly, everything takes
a new face; labor and industry gain life: the merchant becomes more enterprising,
the manufacturer more diligent and skillful, and even the farmer follows his plow
with greater alacrity and attention. * * * It is of no manner of consequence with
regard to the domestic happiness of a state whether money be in a greater or less
quantity. The good policy of the magistrate consists only in keeping it, if possible,
still increasing; because by that means he keeps alive a spirit of industry in the
nation and increases the stock of labor, in which consists all real power and riches.
A nation whose money decreases is actually at that time weaker and more misera-
ble than another nation which possesses no more money, but is on the increasing
hand.

William H. Crawford, Secretary of the Treasury, in a report to
Congress, dated 12th February, 1820, says:

All intelligent writers on currency agree that when it is decreasing in amount
poverty and misery must prevail.

Mr. R. M. T. Hunter, in a report to the United States Senate
in 1852, says:

Of all the great effects produced upon human society by the discovery of America,
there were probably none so marked as those brought about by the great influx
of the precious metals from the New World to the Old. European industry had
been declining under the decreasing stock of the precious metals and an appreciating standard of values; human ingenuity grew dull under the paralyzing influences of declining profits, and capital absorbed nearly all that should have been
divided between it and labor. But an increase of the precious metals, in such
quantity as to check this tendency, operated as a new motive power to the machinery of commerce. Production was stimulated by finding the advantages of a
change in the standard on its side. Instead of being repressed by having to pay
more than it had stipulated for the use of capital, it was stimulated by paying
less. Capital, too, was benefited, for new demands were created for it by the
new uses which a general movement in industrial pursuits had developed; so
that if it lost a little by a change in the standard, it gained much more in the
greater demand for its use, which added to its capacity for reproduction, and to
to its real value.

The mischief would be great, indeed, if all the world were to adopt but one of

JONES

the precious metals as the standard of value. To adopt gold alone would diminish the specie currency more than one-half; and the reduction the other way, should silver be taken as the only standard, would be large enough to prove highly disastrous to the human race.

The Encyclopædia Britannica, 1859 (article Precious Metals, by J. R. McCulloch), says:

A fall in the value of the precious metals, caused by the greater facility of their production, or by the discovery of new sources of supply, depends in no degree on the theories of philosophers or the decision of statesmen or legislators, but is the result of circumstances beyond human control; and although, like a fall of rain after a long course of dry weather, it may be prejudicial to certain classes, it is beneficial to an incomparably greater number, including all who are engaged in industrial pursuits, and is, speaking generally, of great public or national advantage.

Ernest Seyd, 1868 (Bullion, page 613), says:

Upon this one point all authorities on the subject are agreed, to wit, that the large increase in the supply of gold has given a universal impetus to trade, commerce, and industry, and to general social development and progress.

The American Review (1876) says:

Diminishing money and falling prices are not only oppressive upon debtors, of whom, in modern times, states are the greatest, but they cause stagnation in business, reduced production, and enforced idleness. Falling markets annihilate profits, and as it is only the expectation of gain which stimulates the investment of capital in operations, inadequate employment is found for labor, and those who are employed can only be so upon the condition of diminished wages. An increasing amount of money, and consequently augmenting prices, are attended by results precisely the contrary. Production is stimulated by the profits resulting from advancing prices; labor is consequently in demand and better paid, and the general activity and buoyancy insure to capital a wider demand and higher remuneration.

PRICE THE INDEX OF THE VALUE OF MONEY.

There can be no truer index of the value of money than the general range of prices. Price is the mercury by the rise and fall of which the heat and struggle of industrial and business life are daily measured and made plain. Where the tendency of this indicator continues downward, there is no more certain sign that money is increasing in value.

During a period of falling prices the fear of impending calamity hangs like a pall over the business of the country. Notwithstanding unremitting efforts, men feel themselves constantly on the edge of disaster. Gloomy foreboding and timidity take the place of confidence and courage.

A shrinking volume of money is the most insidious foe with which civilization has to contend.

It is my firm conviction that the inexpressible miseries inflicted upon mankind by war, pestilence, and famine have been less cruel, unpitying, and unrelenting than the persistent and remorseless exactions which this inexorable enemy has made upon society. As the volume of money contracts prices decline, and with the decline of prices comes stagnation of industry, and the relegation to idleness of thousands of willing workmen. Capitalists become unwilling to invest their money in enterprises that employ labor while the products of that labor are constantly decreasing in price. During all periods of falling prices therefore money capital is withdrawn from active industry and seeks investment in bonds and other forms of money-futures yielding fixed incomes. For although the rate of interest in many such cases may be low, the capitalist is compensated for this by the enhancement in the purchasing power of each dollar of the principal and by the necessarily greater command it secures over the products of labor.

JONES

Avoiding the very purpose for which it was devised, money at such times seeks seclusion and declines to circulate. Its owner finds that he can better afford to leave it idle in a vault or bury it in the earth, than subject it to the probability of diminution by investing it in business on a constantly falling market. Thus, contrary to all principles of progress and of natural justice, the man who keeps his money idle, and deprives society of its use, is rewarded by an unearned increment, while he who puts his money into active business, where industry and labor may profit by it is punished by unmerited loss.

Under such conditions it is impossible for a community to reach that degree of material progress which, under proper circumstances, it would readily attain. At every turn distress and discouragement stare the people in the face. In every town and village men, willing to work, stand idle. Even their misfortune does not end with themselves, for not only are they a tax upon their friends, lessening to some extent the meager income of those who give them temporary assistance, but their necessary and eager competition for the little work that offers, tends to reduce the compensation of those to whom they are thus indebted. Stores, workshops, and factories, unoccupied and unused, are found in every direction. Crime increases, bankruptcies multiply, and even though the aggregate of wealth augments, it is unjustly distributed, and consequently barren of beneficent results.

A GLANCE AT THE HISTORY OF MONEY.

The system of relying upon the precious metals as money has long been known as the Automatic system. Accurately, it should be called the *Accidental* system. It has been called "automatic" because, so long as money was made to depend solely upon the yield of the mines, the supply regulated itself by what was believed to be a natural method, namely, by the expenditure of labor in its production, and was limited only by the rude obstacles which nature opposes to the production of the metals. The necessity of expending this labor placed the money volume of any country beyond the control of the kings and conquerers who, in the primitive periods of society, exercised despotic sway over their subjects. It was undoubtedly better for the people of those early times to risk the accidents of production than the follies and sinister designs of rulers.

This automatic system grew out of barter. It is a survival from the period when articles were exchanged directly, not for gold and silver as money, but for gold and silver as commodities—on the basis of their cost of production—as in the case of the articles for which they were exchanged.

There have been the same evolutions of progress in money as in all other things. In the rude original of society no kind of money was possible. The first trade was by barter, after which, some one or more commodities attainable in the vicinage, and in general use and demand were selected as the common media through which all exchanges were filtered. The use for that purpose of various metals by weight followed next, and, at a succeeding stage, gold, silver, and copper by weight, and after this their use in the form of coins, the value of which coincided with the bullion-value, which must necessarily be the case when free coinage is permitted.

It may be not uninteresting in this connection to have a general view of the materials which, at different epochs of the world's history, have been used as money. I therefore present a tabular statement giving those particulars in chronological order.

JONES

Table showing some of the substances which have, at various periods and in various countries, been used as money.

Period.	Country.	Substance used as money.	Authority.
B. C. 1900	Palestine	Cattle, and gold and silver, by weight.	The Scriptures.
	Arabia..........	Gold and silver coins.........	Jacob.
	Phœnicia	Gold, silver, and copper coins	Anonymous.
	Phœnician colony in Spain.	Same (some still extant)......	Carter.
1200	Phrygia	Coins, by Queen of Pelops....	Julius Pollux.
1184	Greece..........	Brass coins......	Homer.
862	Argos	Gold and silver coins, by Phidon.	Dictionary of Dates.
700-500	Rome	Brass, by weight	Jacob.
578	Rome	Copper coins.................	Ibid.
Uncertain..	Carthage	Leather or parchment money, first " paper bills " known.	Socrates. Dial. on Riches, Journal des Economistes, 1874, p. 354.
B. C. 491	Sicily	Gold coins, by Gelo (some still extant).	Jacob.
460	Persia	Gold coin, by Darius (two still extant).	Ibid.
478	Sicily	Gold coin, by Hiero (some still extant).	Ibid.
407	Athens	Debased gold coins, foreign...	MacLeod, 476.
400	Sparta	Iron, overvalued	Bœckh.
360	Macedonia......	First gold coins coined in Greece, by Philip.	Jacob.
260	Rome	First silver coins coined in Rome.	Ibid.
54	Britain..........	Pieces of iron	Ibid.
50	Rome	Tin and brass coin............	Dic. of Dates.
Uncertain..	Arabia..........	Glass coins..................	N.Y. Tribune. July 2, 1872.

Period following the failure of the ancient mines.

Period.	Country.	Substance used as money.	Authority.
A. D. 212	Rome. (Caracalla.)	Lead coins silvered, and copper coins gilded.	Anonymous.
		Living money, or human being made a legal tender for debts at about £2 16s. 3d., per capita.	Henry's History of Great Britain, vol. iv, p. 243.
1000	Britain		
1160	Italy............	Paper invented; bills of exchange introduced by the Jews.	Anderson.
1240	Milan, Italy	Paper bills a legal tender	Arthur Young.
1275	China...........	Paper bills a legal tender	Marco Polo.
	Africa, part of..	"Machutes" (ideal money; this view doubted.)	Montesquieu.
1470	Granada, Spain .	Paper bills a legal tender ...	Irving.
1574	Holland	Pasteboard bills, representative.	Dic. of Dates.
Uncertain.	Iceland	Dried fish	Anonymous.
Uncertain.	Newfoundland..	Codfish, dried...............	Anonymous.
Uncertain.	Norway and Greenland.	Seal skins and blubber.......	Anonymous.
Uncertain.	Hindostan and parts of Africa.	Cowry shells	Jacob, 372.

JONES

*Table showing some of the substances used as money—*continued.

*Period following the failure of the ancient mines—*continued.

Period.	Country.	Substance used as money.	Authority.
Uncertain.	North America Indian tribes.	Agate, carnelian, jasper, lead, copper, gold, silver, terracotta, mica, pearl, lignite, coal, bone, shells, chalcedony, wampumpeag, etc.	Anonymous.
Uncertain.	Oriental pastoral tribes.	Cattle, grain, etc...............	Anonymous.
Uncertain.	Abyssinia	Salt	Anonymous.
Uncertain.	China and India.	Rice	Anonymous.
Uncertain.	India............	Paper bills ...., ...	Patterson, p. 13.
Uncertain.	China...........	Pieces of silk cloth...........	Ibid.
Uncertain.	Africa	Strips of cotton cloth.	Ibid.
	Not stated......	Wooden tallies or checks.....	Ibid.

Period following the discovery of the American mines.

A. D. 1631	Massachusetts..	Corn a legal-tender at market prices.	Macgreggor.
1635	Massachusetts..	Musket-balls.................	Anonymous.
1690	Massachusetts..	Paper bills, colonial notes....	Macgreggor.
1694	England........	Bank-notes....................	McCulloch.
1700	Sweden ....'...	Copper and iron coins........	Voltaire's Charles XII.
1702	South Carolina..	Colonial notes................	Macgreggor.
1712	South Carolina..	Bank notes...................	Ibid.
1716	France..........	Inconvertible paper bills a legal tender.	Murray.
1723	Pennsylvania ...	Paper bills, colonial notes....	Macgreggor.
1732	Maryland	Indian corn a legal-tender at 23d. per bushel.	Anonymous.
1732	Maryland.......	Tobacco a legal-tender at 1d. per pound.	Anonymous.
1776	Scotland	Tenpenny nails for small change.	Adam Smith.
1785	Frankland,State of (now part of North Carolina)	Linen at 3s. 6d. per yard, whisky at 2s. 6d. per gallon, and peltry as legal-tender.	Wheeler's History of North Carolina, 94.
1810–1840	All commercial countries.	Great era of bank-paper bills.	
1826	Russia..........	Platinum coins (discontinued in 1845).	App. Encyc.
1847	Mexico, parts of	Cocoa beans; and at Castle of Perote, soap.	Anonymous.

Period following the openings of California and Austrália.

1849	California	Gold dust by weight, also minute gold coins for small change, coined in private mints.	
1855	Australia.......	Gold dust by weight.........	Private information.
185–	Communist settlement in Ohio, called "Utopia."	Paper bills, each representing "one hour's labor."	

JONES

Table showing some of the substances used as money—Continued.

Period following the openings of California and Australia—Continued.

Period.	Country.	Substance used as money.	Authority.
1862	United States ..	Paper bills a legal tender	Act of Feb. 25.
1863	North Carolina .	Tenpenny nails, at 5 cents each, for small change.	Anonymous.
1863	Camp at Florence, S. C.	Potatoes for small change....	Yorkville Enquirer.
1863	United States...	Postage-stamps for small change, temporary.	
1865	Philadelphia, Pa.	Turnips for small change, temporary and local.	Philadelphia Ledger, April
1865	United States...	Nickel coins for small change, overvalued.	Act of March 3.

An analysis of this table will show how carefully even the most primitive communities guarded against a too restricted money volume.

The materials chosen to serve the purpose of money in each country during the early history of society were, it will be observed, such as at the time and place would be of sufficient quantity or volume to insure against any sudden deprivation of supply. In countries where the chase was common, the skins of wild animals were used as money; in maritime communities, shells; in pastoral countries, cattle; in the early history of agriculture, grain; in early mining periods, base metal; in primitive manufacturing ages, nails, glass, musket-balls, strips of cotton, etc.

As communities developed, and commerce between them began, substances somewhat common to all countries, portable and indestructible, such as the precious metals, came to be more, and other substances less, resorted to. By reason of their great beauty those metals were always in demand, even among barbarous peoples, for purposes of ornament and decoration. Because of their universal use for such purposes they came to be recognized as things for which anything else could with safety be exchanged, and as society advanced, and it came to be recognized that some medium should be adopted in which to make all exchanges, those metals were naturally selected for the purpose, so that, together, they became, as it were, a common denominator of value. Their selection proved a convenient method of storing away wealth in a form that commanded at all times every other form of wealth. They had always passed by weight wherever used, but as society became better organized, and its methods more complex, it became necessary, in order to insure against fraud, to form them into pieces convenient for handling, and to invest them distinctly with the function of money, so that, by law, they became a universal solvent for debts and demands, the stamp of the government placed on the coin testifying to its weight and fineness.

Both metals, as shown by the table, have been concurrently used as money for thousands of years—not only since the dawn of history, but from a period anterior to any historical records. The oldest annals show that they had already been employed as circulating media and that their relative values, or the ratio of their exchange for one another, had already been established. Gold and silver were used as money in Palestine as early as the year 1900 B. C. We read in the Bible that Abraham weighed to Ephron the Hittite 400 shekels of silver, "current money with the merchant." An inscription on the temple of Karnak, of the date of 1600 B. C. mentions those metals as materials in which tribute was paid.

But long anterior even to these dates, both metals had been used, as, among the relics of the bronze age of the prehistoric era, ornaments of both gold and silver have been found. Gold, being the, less abundant of the two metals, has had the higher value; but the ratio between the two has been marvelously steady, taking into account the great sweep of ages during which they have been used as money. This will be seen by reference to the following tables of ratios. I will first take their relative values during ancient times.

Table showing the ratio of gold and silver in various countries of the world up to the Christian era.

B. C.	Ratio.	Authorities.
1600	1 to 13.33	Inscriptions at Karnak; tribute lists of Thutmosis. (Brandis.)
708	1 to 13.33	Cuneiform inscriptions on plates found in foundation of Khorsabad.
	1 to 13.33	Ancient Persian coins; gold darics at 8.3 grams = 20 silver siglos, at 5.5 grams.
500	1 to 13.00	Persia. Darius. Egyptian tribute. Herod. III,. 95. (Bœckh, page 12.)
490	1 to 12.50	Sicily. Time of Gelon. "At least" 12.50. (Bœckh, page 44.)
470	1 to 10.00	Doubtful. Asia Minor. Xerxes's treasure. (Bœckh, page 11.)
440	1 to 13.00	Herodotus's account of Indian tributes. 360 gold talents = 4,680 silver.
420	1 to 10.00	Asia Minor. Pay of Xenophon's troops in silver darics. (Anab.; Bœckh. page 34.)
407	1 to ——	Spurious and debased gold coins at Athens. (MacLeod, Polit. Econ., page 475; Bœckh. page 35.)
400	1 to 13.33	Standard in Asia, according to Xenophon.
400	1 to 12.00	Standard in Greece according to "Hipparchus"; attributed to Plato.
400	1 to 12.00	
400	1 to 13.50	Various authorities adduced by Bœckh.
404–336	1 to {12.00 13.00 13.33}	Values in Greece from the Peloponnesian war to the time of Alexander, according to hints in Greek writers. There were variations under special contracts—unit, the silver drachma.
310	1 to 14.00	Greece. Time of Demosthenese. (Bœckh, page 44.)
338–326	1 to 11.50	Special contracts in Greece.
343–323	1 to 12.50	Egypt under the Ptolemies.
300	1 to 10.00	Greece. Continued depression of gold, caused by great influx under Alexander.
207	1 to 13.70	Rome. (Bœckh, page 44.) Gold scriptulum arbitrarily fixed at 17.143 for 1.
100	1 to 11.91	Rome. General rate of gold pound to silver sesterces to date.
58–49	1 to 8.93	Rome. Continued depression of gold, caused by influx of Cæsar's spoil from Gaul. [N. B.—Cæsar's headquarters were at Aquileia, at the head of the Adriatic, where there was also a gold mine, which at this period became very prolific.]
50	1 to 11.90	Rome. "About the year U. C. 700," the rate was 11 19-21. (Bœckh, page 44.)
29	1 to 12.00	Rome. Normal rate in the last days of the republic.

By reference to the foregoing table it will be observed that the increase in the supply of gold in Europe, consisting of the spoils of the Orient, gathered by Alexander the Great, and brought by him to Greece, had the effect of decreasing the value of that metal so that instead of being exchangeable at the ratio of 1 to about 13½ of silver, as formerly, gold became depressed, 1 ounce of it exchanging for only 10 ounces of silver. Later, when Julius Cæsar extended his conquering arms into Gaul, and sent to Rome the accumulations of treasure amassed by him, the value of gold by reason of the increased supply was again depressed, so that an ounce of it was exchangeable for only 8.93 ounces of silver. With these exceptions it may be said that the relation of silver to gold for sixteen hundred years before the time of Christ had varied only from the ratio of 1 to 12 to that of 1 to 13.33. Silver at no time during all this period fell below 13.50 to 1 of gold.

Looking, now, at the relative values of gold and silver from the time of Christ to the discovery of America, we find the ratio between the two metals to be as follows:

Table showing the ratio of gold and silver in various countries of the world from the opening of the Christian era to the discovery of America:

A. D.	Ratio.	Authorities.
1–37	1 to 10. 97	Rome. Rate under Augustus and Tiberius.
37–41	1 to 12. 17	Rome. Reign of Caligula.
54–68	1 to 11. 80	Rome. Reign of Nero.
69–79	1 to 11. 54	Rome. Reign of Vespasian.
81–96	1 to 11. 30	Rome. Reign of Domitian.
138–161	1 to 11. 98	Rome. Reign of Antoninus.
312	1 to 14. 40	Byzantium Reign of Constantine. Arbitrary.
438	1 to 14. 40	Byzantium and Rome. Theodosian code. Arbitrary.
864	1 to 12. 00	Probable ratio, as shown by the Edictum Pistense, under the Carlovingian dynasty
1260	1 to 10. 50	Average ratio in the commercial cities of Italy. Local or doubtful.
1314–1660	1 to ——	England. Numerous mint indentures given in McLeod's Political Economy, page 475. The ratio, except when fixed arbitrarily and in violation of market price, varied between about 1.12 and 1.14 during the two hundred and fifty-seven years included in this period.
1351	1 to 12. 30	
1375	1 to 12. 40	Ratio in North Germany as shown by the very accurate
1403	1 to 12. 80	rules of the Lubeck mint, corroborated in the main by
1411	1 to 12. 00	the accounts of the Teutonic Order of Knights, aver-
1451	1 to 11. 70	aged in periods of forty years.
1463	1 to 11. 60	
1453–1494	1 to 10. 50	Ratio according to the accounts of the Teutonic knights. As the ratio fixed in England by numerous mint in-dentures from 1465 to 1509 was about 1.12 this German ratio is considered local or doubtful.

The annotation for the Roman reigns (1-37 to 138-161) reads: "The silver coinage much debased, consequently the ratio of the metals pure was about 1 to 11."

It will thus be observed that during the one thousand four hundred and ninety-two years from the coming of Christ to the discovery of America, silver never went below the ratio of 14.40 to one of gold.

The relations which the metals have borne to each other since the discovery of the New World will appear from the following:

JONES

Table showing the relative values of gold and silver in the various countries of the world from the discovery of America to 1630.

A. D.	Ratio.	Authorities.
1497	1 to 10.70	Spain. Reign of Isabella. Edict of Medina. Local.
1500	1 to 10.50	Germany. Adam Riese's Arithmetic. Local or doubtful.
1551	1 to 11.17	Germany. Imperial mint regulations. Arbitrary or local.
1559	1 to 11.44	German Imperial mint regulations.
1561	1 to 11.70	France. Mint regulations.
1575	1 to 11.68	
1623	1 to 11.74	Upper Germany. Mint regulations.
1640	1 to 13.51	France. Mint regulations. Transition period.
1665	1 to 15.10	France. Mint regulations.
1667	1 to 14.15	Upper Germany. Mint regulations. Doubtful.
1669	1 to 15 11	Upper Germany. Mint regulations.
1679	1 to 15.00	France. Mint regulations.
1680	1 to 15.40	

Table showing the ratio of silver to 1 of gold from 1687 to the demonetization of silver by Germany and the United States and the closing of the Mints to its free coinage.

[From the Report (1890) of the Director of the U. S. Mint on the Production of the Precious Metals in the United States.]

[NOTE.—From 1687 to 1832 the ratios are taken from Dr. A. Soetbeer; from 1833 to 1878 from Pixley and Abell's tables; and from 1879 to 1889 from daily cablegrams from London to the Bureau of the Mint.]

Year.	Ratio.	Year.	Ratio.	Year.	Ratio.	Year.	Ratio.
1687	14.94	1721	15.05	1755	14.68	1789	14.75
1688	14.94	1722	15.17	1756	14.94	1790	15.04
1689	15.02	1723	15.20	1757	14.87	1791	15.05
1690	15.02	1724	15.11	1758	14.85	1792	15.17
1691	14.98	1725	15.11	1759	14.15	1793	15.00
1692	14.92	1726	15.15	1760	14.14	1794	15.37
1693	14.83	1727	15.24	1761	14.54	1795	15.55
1694	14.87	1728	15.11	1762	15.27	1796	15.65
1695	15.02	1729	14.92	1763	14.99	1797	15.41
1696	15.00	1730	14.81	1764	14.70	1798	15.59
1697	15.20	1731	14.94	1765	14.83	1799	15.74
1698	15.07	1732	15.09	1766	14 80	1800	15.68
1699	14.94	1733	15.18	1767	14.85	1801	15.46
1700	14.81	1734	15.39	1768	14.80	1802	15.26
1701	15.07	1735	15.41	1769	14.72	1803	15.41
1702	15.52	1736	15.18	1770	14.62	1804	15.41
1703	15.17	1737	15.02	1771	14.66	1805	15.79
1704	15.22	1738	14.91	1772	14.52	1806	15.52
1705	15.11	1739	14.91	1773	14.62	1807	15.43
1706	15.27	1740	14.94	1774	14.62	1808	16.08
1707	15.44	1741	14.92	1775	14.72	1809	15.96
1708	15.41	1742	14.85	1776	14.55	1810	15.77
1709	15.31	1743	14.85	1777	14.54	1811	15.53
1710	15.22	1744	14.87	1778	14.68	1812	16.11
1711	15.29	1745	14.98	1779	14.80	1813	16.25
1712	15.31	1746	15.13	1780	14.72	1814	15.04
1713	15.24	1747	15.26	1781	14.78	1815	15.26
1714	15.13	1748	15.11	1782	14.42	1816	15.28
1715	15.11	1749	14.80	1783	14.48	1817	15.11
1716	15.09	1750	14.55	1784	14.70	1818	15.35
1717	15.13	1751	14.39	1785	14.92	1819	15.33
1718	15.11	1752	14.54	1786	14.96	1820	15.62
1719	15.09	1753	14.54	1787	14.92	1821	15.95
1720	15.04	1754	14.48	1788	14.65	1822	15.80

JONES

Year.	Ratio.	Year.	Ratio.	Year.	Ratio.	Year.	Ratio.
1823	15.84	1836	15.72	1849	15.78	1861	15.50
1824	15.82	1837	15.83	1850	15.70	1862	15.35
1825	15.70	1838	15.85	1851	15.46	1863	15.37
1826	15.76	1839	15.62	1852	15.59	1864	15.37
1827	15.74	1840	15.62	1853	15.33	1865	15.44
1828	15.78	1841	15.70	1854	15.33	1866	15.43
1829	15.78	1842	15.87	1855	15.38	1867	15.57
1830	15.82	1843	15.93	1856	15.38	1868	15.59
1831	15.72	1844	15.85	1857	15.27	1869	15.60
1832	15.73	1845	15.92	1858	15.38	1870	15.57
1833	15.93	1846	15.90	1859	15.19	1871	15.57
1834	15.73	1847	15.80	1860	15.29	1872	15.63
1835	15.80	1848	15.85				

By the foregoing table it will be seen that in the three hundred and seventy-five years from 1497 to 1872 the maximum separation of the metals was only as 1 to 16.25—notwithstanding the widest divergencies during that long period in the yield of the two metals from the mines. It will be observed that all the later quotations are from the London market, but it is a significant fact that in France, where, by the law of 7 Germinal, An XI, (1803,) free coinage was permitted to both metals, at the ratio of 15½ of silver to 1 of gold, for a period of seventy years, and until the coinage of silver was limited, there was at no time the slightest variance from that relation.

When silver was deprived of the full money function, and all the money-work of society was placed on gold, the metals began to separate. The following table shows the degree of that separation from year to year:

Table showing the ratio of silver to 1 of gold since the demonetization of silver by Germany and the United States, and the closing of all mints of the western world to its free coinage:

1873	15.92	1882	18.19
1874	16.17	1883	18.64
1875	16.59	1884	18.57
1876	17.88	1885	19.41
1877	17.22	1886	20.78
1878	17.94	1887	21.13
1879	18.40	1888	21.99
1880	18.05	1889	22.10
1881	18.16		

The foregoing figures show that it is only since the legislative proscription of silver by Germany and the United States, and the closing of all the European mints to its coinage, that any material change took place in the ratio between the two metals, which conclusively demonstrates that the present divergence in the relative values of the two metals is directly due to the legal outlawry of silver and not to natural causes.

Not only has the concurrent use of the two metals as money had the sanction of all time, but the approval of the greatest minds of history, and, when not blinded by self-interest, the approval of practical and experienced financial minds. So well recognized is this fact that I need only cite a few instances of such approval.

Alexander Hamilton said:

To annul the use of either of the metals as money is to abridge the quantity of circulating medium, and is liable to all the objections which arise from a comparison of the benefits of a full with the evils of a scanty circulation. (Report to Congress, 1791.)

JONES

Thomas Jefferson, in a letter to Hamilton, indorsed this view, saying:

I return you the report on the mint. I concur with you that the unit *must stand on both meta s.* (Letter to Hamilton, February, 1792.)

In his "Recherches sur l'or et sur l'argent," 1843, Léon Fauchet said:

If all the nations of Europe adopted the system of Great Britain, the price of gold would be raised beyond measure, and we should see produced in Eur pe a most lamentable result. The Government can not decree that legal tender shall be only gold, in place of silver, for that would be to decree a revolution, and the most dangerous of all, because it would be a revolution leading to unknown results (*qui marcherait vers l'inconnu*).

In a memoir read before the French Institute in 1868, M. Wolowski said:

The suppression of silver would bring on a veritable revolution. Gold would augment in value with a rapid and constant progress, which would break the faith of contracts nd aggravate the situation of all debtors, including the nation. It would add at one stroke of the pen at least three milliards to the twelve milliards of the public debt.

In a debate in the French Senate on January 28, 1870, Senator Dumas eloquently pleaded for caution in dealing with a subject of such farreaching importance as the demonetization of one of the money metals. He said:

Those who approach these questions for the first time decide them at once. Those who study them with care hesitate. Those who are obliged practically to decide doubt and stop, overwhelmed with the weight of the enormous responsibility.

The quantities of the precious metals which are now sufficient may become insufficient, and we should proceed with great prudence before we diminish that which constitutes a part of the riches of the human race. Sometimes gold takes the place of silver. Sometimes silver takes the place of gold. *This keeps up the general equilibrium.* Nobody can guaranty that the present vast production of gold will continue. The *placers* are found on the surface of the earth, and may be exhausted by the very facility of working them. Silver presents itself in the form of subterranean veins. Science may contribute to accelerate its extraction. In presence of the unknown, which dominates the future, we should practice a prudent reserve.

Before a French monetary convention in 1869 testimony was given by M. Wolowski, by Baron Rothschild, and by M. Rouland, governor of the Bank of France.

M. Wolowski said:

The sum total of the precious metals is reckoned at fifty milliards, one-half gold and one-half silver. If, by a stroke of the pen, they suppress one of these metals in the monetary service, they double the demand for the other metal, to the ruin of all debtors.

M. Rouland, governor of the Bank of France, said:

We have not to do with ideal theories. The two moneys have actually co-existed since the origin of human society. They co-exist because the two together are necessary, by their quantity, to meet the needs of circulation. This necessity of the two metals, has it ceased to exist? Is it established that the quantity of actual and prospective gold is such that we can now renounce the use of silver without disaster?

Baron Rothschild said:

The simultaneous employment of the two precious metals is satisfactory and gives rise to no complaint. Whether gold or silver dominates for the time being, it is always true that the two metals concur together in forming the monetary circulation of the world, and it is the general mass of the two metals combined which serves as the measure of the value of things. The suppression of silver would amount to a veritable destruction of values without any compensation.

JONES——2

At the session (October 30, 1873) of the Belgian Monetary Commission, Professor Laveleye, one of the most luminous writers on economic subjects, said:

Debtors, and among them the state, have the right to pay in gold or silver, and this right can not be taken away without disturbing the relation of debtors and creditors, to the prejudice of debtors, to the extent of perhaps one-half, certainly of one-third. To increase all debts at a blow (*brusquement*) is a measure so violent, so revolutionary, that I can not believe that the Government will propose it or that the Chambers will vote it.

WHY WAS THE AUTOMATIC SYSTEM INTERFERED WITH?

Some thirteen years ago, as Chairman of the Monetary Commission appointed by Congress to investigate the causes of the changes in the relative values of the precious metals, I submitted to this body a report, in which I took occasion to refer to the motives which evidently influenced the creditor classes of the western world in destroying the automatic system of money. From that Report I quote as follows:

The world has generally favored, theoretically if not practically, the automatic metallic system, and adjusted its business to it. Some nations adopted one metal as their standard, and some the other, and some adopted both. Those that adopted both metals served as a balance-wheel to steady with exactness their relative value. The practical effect of all of this was the same as if all nations had adopted both, because it secured the entire stock of both at a fixed equivalency for the transaction of the business of the world. While some nations have changed their money metal, or, having bad paper money, have resumed specie payments in one metal, the policy of a general demonetization of one of the metals was first broached only about twenty years ago. About ten years later a formidable propaganda was organized to fasten that policy upon the commercial world.

This new school of financial theorists advocate the retention of metal as the material of money, but favor its subjection to governmental interference in every respect. Whenever new mines are discovered, or old ones yield or promise to yield more abundantly, instead of freely accepting their product in accordance with the automatic theory, they advocate its rejection through the restriction or the absolute prohibition of the coinage of either or both metals, or through the limitation or the abolition of the legal-tender function of one of them. Whenever the interests of the creditor and income classes seem to be in danger of being impaired by an increase in the volume and decrease in the value of money, or in other words, by a general rise in prices, these modern theorists are clamorous in double-standard countries for the demonetization of one of the money metals, and in single-standard countries for the shifting of the money function from the metal which promises the most to the one that promises the least abundant supply. They are extremely anxious for the retention of the *material* of which the money-standard is composed when such material is rising in value and prices are falling, and exceedingly apprehensive of the evil and inconvenience which they predict as sure to result from changing it.

Whenever a fall in prices occurs, through either a natural or artificial contraction in the volume of money, they maintain that it is due to antecedent inflation and extravagance, or to overproduction through persistent and reckless industry; if the contraction be natural, that it can not be helped, and if artificial, that though it may inflict great temporary losses on the masses of the people, it will be sure to result in their ultimate benefit, and they console the sufferers with the comforting assurance that such contraction is necessary in order to reach the lowest depths of that "*hard pan*" whose foundations they have previously undermined by demonetizing one of the metals, and upon which alone they claim that money, capital, and labor can securely and harmoniously rest. But when the material composing the standard is falling in value and prices are rising, they immediately discover that the maintenance of the *value* of the standard is the all-important consideration, and that its material is of no importance whatever and should be at once changed to "*redress the situation*." After having reduced one of the metals to a commodity by depriving it of the money function, these theorists complacently point to the resulting fluctuations in its value as a justification of the act producing them, and as a conclusive proof of the unfitness for money of the demonetized metal. * * *

Metallic money, on this theory, is no longer automatic, but is as completely subjected to government control for all injurious purposes as paper money. But, unlike paper money, the control over this kind of metallic money can only be exercised in the baneful direction of decreasing its volume, and thereby making property cheaper and money scarcer and dearer.

JONES

This is a one-sided system, which can operate only in the interest of the security creditor, the usurer, and pawnbroker, whom it enables, through the falling prices which itself occasions, to swallow up the shrunken resources of the debtor, but is impotent to protect the interests of the unsecured business creditor, the debtor, or society, when, from any cause, the supply of the money metals becomes deficient.

The world has expended a vast amount of labor in the production of the precious metals, and has made great sacrifices in upholding the automatic metallic system of money, and has a right to insist that it shall be consistently let alone to work out its own conclusions, or that it be abandoned.

The history of the subsequent struggle to remonetize silver only serves to illustrate and emphasize the correctness of that statement of the case.

Between 1810 and 1849, according to Tooke and Newmarch (recognized authorities on the subject), gold increased in value 145 per cent. which is equivalent to a fall in the general range of prices of 59 per.cent. No movement was then made or suggestion offered by the debtors, or by any class of the community, to add any new money-metal to the metals already in use, with the view of increasing the volume of money, so that the equity of time contracts might be maintained, and the value of the unit of money kept at a steady and unchanging level.

But as soon as the discoveries of gold were made in the alluvial deposits of California and Australia, or rather as soon as it was suspected that money would thereby become considerably increased in volume, the annuitants and income classes, the creditors everywhere, took steps to avert what they characterized as a great calamity. They openly declared their purpose, by every means in their power, to prevent a decline in the value of money, so that the purchasing power of their incomes might not be reduced. They determined to go to any length in order to prevent the rise of prices which their aggressive instincts led them to fear would follow the additions to the money volume of the world by the natural and much needed yield of the mines.

The fiat therefore went forth that one of the metals must be discarded.

THE PROPOSITION FIRST MADE TO DEMONETIZE GOLD.

If anything were needed to demonstrate that the reason for the demonetization of silver was the cupidity of the creditor classes—the money-lenders, annuitants, and those in receipt of fixed incomes—and that it was not any defect inhering in the metal silver, nor any change in its adaptability to subserve the purposes of money, it is to be found in the significant fact that the metal first selected for demonetization was not silver but gold—that metal which has since become the idol of the money-changers, and which is now declared to be the only "natural" money. The openly-avowed determination was to increase the value of money, and in order to accomplish that purpose the metal which promised the largest yield was to be condemned and stripped of its ancient monetary function. So strongly was this determination set forth, so earnestly was it presented, and so urgently pressed on the ground of duty that its achievement came to be regarded as the fulfillment of a high moral purpose.

It was with gold then as it came to be with silver afterward, and as it always is with whatever interferes with the interests of privileged classes, intrenched in power and prerogative,—the determination to destroy it being arrived at, measures were taken to prove that the public good required its destruction. While the purpose was to discard the metal, whether gold or silver, which threatened most immediately and seriously to reduce the purchasing power of

JONES

money, the argument was that a decrease in the purchasing power of money was a calamity against the happening of which every energy should be directed.

The privileged classes found then, as they find now, able and ingenious advocates and defenders among the literary and educated guilds of the period. The celebrated De Quincy, in England, attempted to prove, and to his own satisfaction did prove upon figures drawn from his fears and a brilliant imagination, that the least yield of gold to be expected from the mines of California and Australia for an indefinite period in the future, was the yearly sum of $350,000,000.

M. Chevalier, in France, vehemently proclaimed the necessity of discarding one of the money metals, and that one not silver but gold. In his work upon the " Fall of Gold " M. Chevalier, in 1856, said :

The quantity of gold annually thrown on the general market approaches in round numbers a milliard of francs ($200,000,000). These two countries (California and Australia) must yet for a long series of years produce gold in such quantities and on such conditions as to render a marked decline in its value inevitable.

It is absolutely certain that so vast a production should be accompanied with a great reduction in value.

In no direction can a new outlet be seen sufficiently large to absorb the extraordinary production of gold which we are now witnessing, so as to prevent a fall in its value.

Unless, then, we possess a very robust faith in the immobility of human affairs, we must regard the fall in the value of gold as an event for which we should prepare without loss of time.

The " preparation " which Chevalier advocated was the discarding of that metal which gave promise of the greatest abundance. He did not attempt to hide his purpose. He boldly stated that his object was to enhance the value of money. This object was also clearly expressed on a later occasion by another distinguished advocate of dear money, Mr. Victor Bonnet, of France, in the Journal des Economistes. He said:

The world is now saturated with the precious metals, and if there is any danger again t which it is necessary to guard, it is that this saturation should become greater. * * *

If the annual production of gold is now reduced to 500,000,000 francs, let us thank Heaven for it, and let us wish that it may not be too rapidly increased, whereby we should be embarrassed. It is the too great abundance and not the scarcity of metallic money which is to be apprehended.

GOLD DEMONETIZED.

In 1857 the German states and Austria demonetized gold ; and had it not been for the opposition of France, which insisted on retaining the double standard, the movement might have become general on the continent. With England, however, nothing could be done. More than a generation had passed since it had declared for the single standard of gold, and its creditors and income classes—the shrewdest, most adept, and watchful of financiers—did not believe that the large yields of gold would long continue.

The creditor classes of the continent, finding England immovable and realizing that the object sought by the English creditors was identical with their own, namely, the increase in the value of money and the depression of prices, concluded that the common purpose could be as well served by the demonetization of one as by that of the other. This conclusion was emphasized by developments on the Comstock lode whose bountiful and beneficent yield of silver was the fitting supplement to the great discoveries of gold on the Pacific coast. The danger of a decline in the value of money was more imminent than ever. The annuitants became alarmed. Commissions were sent from Europe to the Pacific coast to investigate the subject. The United States, too, sent a commissioner to examine into the condition and prospects of the Comstock, and, imbued with many of the characteristics of De Quincey and Chevalier, the United States commissioner, in 1866, reported that if all other mines were worked with the machinery used on the Comstock "their yield would flood the world."

Like many of the present opponents of silver he was endowed with the gift of prophecy, and accordingly we find him confidently predicting that ether and innumerable rich lodes of silver would be found on the Pacific coast which would be worked with great profit. The attack on gold was immediately changed to a combined attack on silver. From that period till the present no means have been left untried to belittle and degrade that metal, and also to disparage those who are in favor of continuing it as one of the money metals of the world.

It was then announced with all the dogmatism of authority that silver was unfit to be used as money. Defects were suddenly discovered in it that the scrutiny of three thousand years had failed to disclose. Its weight and bulk were found to be insuperable obstacles to its use as money. Yet the specific gravity of silver is no greater now than it has been for all the ages during which it has been used as money by all mankind, nor is it any heavier or more bulky than it was in 1851 or 1857, when Belgium, Germany, and Austria demonetized gold and made the "heavy," "bulky," and "inconvenient" metal, silver, their only money metal. Silver can now be transported from place to place with less risk and at no greater expense than gold, and at much less cost than at any previous period in the history of the world.

The objection that silver is too heavy for the pocket is an objection common to all metallic money. We see hardly any gold in circulation in this country—infinitely less than of silver. When our people have a choice as to the form in which they will take money they prefer paper representatives as being the most convenient. The extraordinary perfection to which the arts of the engraver and paper maker have been brought gives paper money a security against counterfeiting and imitation far superior to any immunity which can be claimed for the metals. The marvellous inventions of modern times in the form of safes and vault-locks render it a matter of practically no risk to store the metals, both silver and gold, so that paper representatives of them may be issued. These representatives are preferred by the general mass of the people, and have almost entirely occupied the channels of circulation to the exclusion of both metals. A silver certificate for $1,000 weighs no more than a gold certificate for the same amount.

THE MOTIVE FOR DEMONETIZING SILVER.

The motive for the demonetization of silver was precisely the same that had previously inspired the demonetization of gold. The object was to demonetize one of the metals—that metal which promised the greatest abundance, and which would contribute most largely to maintaining at an equitable level the general range of prices. The motive in both cases was to aggrandize the privileged classes—the income and the creditor classes of the world—and by means of a subtle and sinister manipulation of the money volume, whose effects it is not always easy to trace to their true cause, to practically confiscate the reward of the hard toil of the masses. To all intent and purpose the design was to establish a new system of

slavery for the western world, of which the debtor classes among the
white races should be the victims.

When demonetization was determined on there was no pretense
that there was any difficulty in maintaining a parity between the two
metals at the established ratio.

In the official résumé of the doings of the French monetary commission of 1869 the arguments upon both sides were summed up.

In behalf of the gold standard it was said:

The rise in price which has taken place within twenty years in a great number
of articles of merchandise is evidently due to many causes, such as war, bad
harvests, and increase in consumption; but it is very probable that the depreciation of the precious metals has contributed to it, since there has been a striking
coincidence between the rise of prices and the production of the new mines of
gold and silver. The annual production of the two metals, which was only
$80,000,000 in 1847, exceeds now $200,000,000. It has nearly tripled, and it is easy
to see that the real value of the metals has diminished. It is difficult to estimate
exactly what the diminution is, but whatever it may be it demands the attention of governments, because it affects unfavorably all that portion of the population whose income, remaining nominally the same, undergoes a yearly diminution of purchasing power. As governments control the weight and standard of
money, they ought so far as possible to assure its value. And as it is admitted
that the tendency of the metals is to depreciate, this tendency should be arrested
by demonetizing one of them

In behalf of the double standard it was replied as follows:

Many economists argue that the precious metals, having become very abundant,
have lost 10 or 15 per cent. of their value, and that the situation must be redressed
by making money scarcer by demonetizing silver. To this it may be answered
that the great discoveries of gold of the last twenty years have injured nobody.
The new mass of gold, spreading over the whole world, has found employment in
stimulating all forms of business, and, as a consequence, the value of gold has
fallen very little. According to Mr. Newmarch, the mass of gold and silver has
augmented 3 per cent. per annum, while the mass of exchanges has augmented
more than 3 per cent. per annum, so that the equilibrium has been maintained.
And the present is an especially inopportune time to demonetize silver, because
the annual production of gold has been falling off for several years. It was
$200,000,000 in 1853, and it is now not more than $140,000,000. What will happen
to the civilized world if silver is demonetized and if gold shall then fail?

THE MOTIVE OF ENGLAND.

England did not adopt the gold standard until she was in a position to become the principal creditor nation. When her forges,
furnaces, spindles, and looms were ready to supply manufactured
goods to all the world, she saw that all countries and peoples would
be compelled to pour their treasures into her lap. Her insular
position and great navy guarantied her against external assault.
Released from the anxieties and labors incident to the Napoleonic
wars, with a sturdy population of trained mechanics, and with
fields of coal and iron in abundance, she was well adapted to become
the "workshop of the world." With colonial possessions in every
sea, and with Continental Europe in ceaseless unrest, England could
rely on customers who could themselves produce nothing but raw
material and would be obliged to buy her finished products.

The field of industry had been recently broadened by basic inventions of unparalleled importance—the steam-engine, the power loom,
the spinning-jenny, and a multiplicity of other devices that increased
a hundred fold the efficiency of artisan labor. England knew that
her trade would in the main be a foreign trade and her financial
dealings largely with foreign governments. She knew that from the
people of the continent, impoverished by years of struggle for existence against the attacks of Napoleon, she could not expect immediate
payments in cash, or in commodities. Time bonds and other deferred obligations were the media in which for the most part she
received pay, she made interest and principal payable in gold alone,

JONES

and if before the date of payment the value of money should increase it would not be to the disadvantage of the creditor. Whatever we may think of the *ethics* of this policy, wo can have no difficulty in understanding its *motive*.

As to the object which England had in view in demonetizing silver we are left in no sort of doubt. It has been candidly admitted by many of her financiers and publicists. The reason for her stolid adherence to the gold standard now is the same for which she originally demonetized silver. Her income and creditor classes are daily in receipt of an unearned increment to their wealth by reason of that demonetization. More candid than the advocates in this country of the single gold standard, the writers and press of Great Britain openly avow the object. No better testimony to the fact can be adduced than that supplied by the royal commission appointed in 1836 to inquire into the changes in the relative values of the precious metals. At page 90, Part II, of the final report of that body, section 123, the commission say :

It must be remembered, too, that this country is largely a creditor country, of debts payable in gold, and any change which entails a rise in the price of commodities generally; that is to say, a diminution of the purchasing power of gold would be to our disadvantage.

Before the British Royal Commission of 1868 on International Coinage, Mr. Jacob Behren, an eminent British merchant and member of the Associated Chambers of Commerce, after answering special and technical questions, was asked, in conclusion, "if there was anything else he wished to state." His reply was (p. 13):

I would only state that. in my opinion, the general introduction of gold all over the world has been one of the greatest possible blessings to England. I believe that England would bo now the very poorest country in the world if the silver standard abroad had been kept np, and gold had not been generally introduced. Gold would otherwise have been very much reduced in value, and we should have had all the gold poured into England. All the debts owing to us would have been paid in the depreciated currency; and, therefore, I believe that England ought to have taken the lead in the introduction of a gold onrrency abroad. We ought to be very thankful that it has been introduced, and we ought to give every facility to its circulation.

Sir Lyon Playfair, in a speech delivered in the English Parliament on April 18, 1890, according to the report in the London Times of the day following, said that—

The true policy of England as the chief creditor nation of the world was to keep perfect independence, and to refuse participation in any entangling conference on our monetary system.

And, according to the same report, Sir Lyon Playfair, referring to the holding of the metals together by law, said that—

It was quite true that, if you yoked a cart-horse to a racer, the strength of both would be increased but the speed of the racer would be sacrificed.

Gold is the "racer" whose "speed" must not be sacrificed, no matter how much injury may be effected by its tendency to greater and greater gain.

The weight of the enormous burden which is imposed on gold can not be better illustrated than by a statement of this same Sir Lyon Playfair, made in the same speech. According to the London Times of April 19, he said that—

The liabilities of the banks of Great Britain to the public amounted to £621,-000,000, or about the amount of the national debt of England; but the amount of coin or bullion to meet this liability was only £35,000.000; or, deducting from each side of the account £8,000,000 locked up in the Notes Department of the Bank of England/ it was £27,000,000; or only 4½ per cent. of liabilities.

JONES

24

On the same occasion Mr. Goschen, Chancellor of the Exchequer, delivered an able speech, in which he gave his facts, his eloquence, and his logic to the struggling masses of his countrymen by maintaining the wisdom of remonetization of silver, but gave his conclusions and his policy to the creditor classes by recommending no disturbance of present conditions.

I have contended—

said the Chancellor of the Exchequer—

and am prepared still to contend, that I should prefer the currency of the world to depend upon two metals rather than upon one metal. To those views I gave expression in 1878. * * * I have always looked upon silver and gold not as antagonistic to each other; not as being metals the price of one of which would necessarily fall when the other rose, but I have looked upon them as partners who together were doing the work of the currency of the world.

The English creditor classes have not been without able coadjutors in this country. We have noticed for the last twelve or fourteen years that zealous advocates of the gold standard, the advantages of which are not confined to Great Britain, are to be found among the creditor classes of the United States.

If the toilers of this country, from the proceeds of whose labor these exactions have to be paid, had as little influence on the legislation of the United States as the toilers of England have on the legislation of that country, the creditor classes and financiers of the United States might be as frank as those of Great Britain in admitting the object of maintaining the single gold standard.

How graphically, though unintentionally, does the English poet. Waller, in the following verse, express the advantage which the gold standard gives to creditors everywhere, and the self-satisfaction with which they contemplate life :

> The taste of hot Arabia's spice we know,
> Free from the scorching sun that makes it grow.
> Without the worm, in Persia's silk we shine,
> And without planting, drink of every vine,
> To dig for wealth we weary not our limbs,
> Gold, though the heaviest metal, hither swims.
> Ours is the harvest where the Indians mow,
> We plow the deep, and reap what others sow.

THE MOTIVE OF GERMANY.

When Germany, intoxicated by her victory over France, and in order to further cripple a fallen foe from whom she had exacted $1,000,000,000 in gold, demonetized silver, she inflicted on her people by the fall of prices consequent on the increase in the value of money, more misery than all her armies of horse and foot had been able to inflict on France. France, on the contrary, notwithstanding this unprecedented war tribute, by keeping a sufficient volume of money in circulation to maintain, and even advance, her range of prices, emerged in a few years from the consequences of the greatest disaster in her history, conscious of a triumph more complete than Germany had achieved by all the military splendor of the war. The ransom exacted of France was received back by her almost as soon as paid, in exchange for the products of her industry. It is not a sign of prosperity, Mr. President, when hundreds of thousands of people, the best bone and sinew of a nation, are found annually emigrating ; and it is a coincidence which I merely mention, in passing, that as soon as the effects of demonetization of silver had had time to make themselves felt in Germany, a veritable hegira of its people took place.

JONES

From 1373 to 1889, the emigration from Germany numbered 1,546,-000 persons.

Students of social science everywhere recognize the statistics of illegitimacy and of suicides as among the most powerful evidences of monetary distress. By reference to those statistics we find that notwithstanding the large emigration during that period the number of illegitimate births in Germany increased from 161,294 in 1883 to 169,-645 in 1888. The suicides in Prussia, Bavaria, Saxony, and Baden—the leading states of the German Empire—increased from 179 for each million of population in 1868 to 196 for each million of the population in 1876 and to 218 for each million of the population in 1882. In Prussia alone the number of suicides in 1876 was 151 per million, while in 1882 it was 191 per million.

This is part of the price which the toiling masses of Germany are paying for the gold standard experiment, which, without their consent their imperial government foisted upon them.

Bismarck made the mistake that many able men in all countries of the western world have made and continue to make, namely, that of attributing the commanding position of Great Britain in the commercial and industrial world to her adoption of the gold standard. Bismarck mistook for cause and effect what was a mere coincidence, the result of exceptional conditions, as did those of our legislators in 1873, who happened to know anything whatever of the nature of the act demonetizing silver. The belief of some of the most far-sighted statesmen of Great Britain has been that she secured her position, not by reason of the gold standard, but in spite of it.

In a speech delivered at Glasgow, in November, 1873, after the alteration by Germany in her monetary standard, Mr. Disraeli said:

The monetary disturbance which has occurred, and is now to a certain extent acting very injuriously upon trade, I attribute to the great changes which the Governments of Europe are making in reference to their standard of value. Our gold standard is not the cause of our commercial prosperity, but the consequence of that prosperity. It is quite evident that we must prepare ourselves for great convulsions in the money market, not occasioned by speculation or any of the old causes which have been alleged, but by a new cause with which we are not sufficiently acquainted.

And again in March, 1879, when the effects of the decreasing volume of money were making themselves more and more felt, Mr. Disraeli, then Lord Beaconsfield, said:

All this time the produce of the gold mines of Australia and California has been regularly diminishing, and the consequence is that, while these great alterations on the continent in favor of a gold currency have been made, notwithstanding that increase of population which alone requires a considerable increase of currency to carry on its transactions, the amount of the currency itself is yearly diminishing, until a state of affairs has been brought about by gold production exactly the reverse of that which it produced at first. Gold is every day appreciating in value, and as it appreciates the lower become prices. It is not impossible that, as affairs develop, the country may require that some formal investigation should be made of the causes which are affecting the value of the precious metals, and the effect which the change in the value of the precious metals has upon the industries of the country, and upon the continual fall of prices.

In reaching their conclusions, Bismarck and others ignored the fundamental principle that a gold supply that might be sufficient for one country with a gold standard, and might even result in a measure of prosperity to that country, would be wholly insufficient if other countries should adopt the same standard and should enter upon a keen competition and rivalry for the acquisition of gold.

The adoption of that standard by Germany and France was therefore not only destructive of their own prosperity, but was a stunning blow at the prosperity of England and all other gold-using

JONES

countries. In taking England for his model, Bismarck had not the condition of the toiling masses before his mind, but the glamour of prosperity which surrounded the creditor-barons.

The unprejudiced observer can not fail to perceive that the $370,-000,000 coined under the Limited Coinage Act of the United States of 1878, supplementing the gold stock of the western world, postponed great industrial and financial crises. But the elements of these crises are gathering, and, unless relief be soon forthcoming, will burst upon the world with crushing severity.

DEMONETIZATION IN THE UNITED STATES.

If we are surprised that the sordid selfishness of the privileged classes of Europe should have induced them to perpetrate so gross an act of injustice, we are reminded that the legislation of monarchical countries has usually been controlled in the interest of the privileged classes. But what shall be said in defense of the demonetization of silver by the United States? No such stupendous act of folly and injustice was ever before perpetrated by the representatives of a free people.

Our position differed materially from that of Great Britain. This was not a creditor nation. Our people did not, and do not, own thousands of millions of dollars of foreign bonds, on which to receive semi-annual interest in a constantly appreciating money, which would have to be paid from the current earnings of foreign labor. Instead, therefore, of our demonetization unjustly enriching our creditor-classes at the expense of foreigners, it enabled the creditors at home here to rob and despoil the debtors among their own countrymen. Instead of despoiling the Canadian, the Australian, the East Indian, the Egyptian, or the Turk, the spoliation arranged for by our adoption of the gold standard was a spoliation of the debtors in our own communities. In so far, however, as our debt was held abroad, it provided for a spoliation of our citizens by the foreign bondholders also. And as nearly all our public debt was so held, we had presented to us in 1873 the extraordinary spectacle of representatives, sent here to enact laws for the welfare and advancement of our own people, devoting all their energies, whether aware of it or not, to the upbuilding of the fortunes of the moneyed aristocracies of other countries, at the expense of the producers of the United States.

CONDITION OF THE COUNTRY AT THE TIME.

Consider for a moment the condition of this country at the time when this amazing piece of legislation was enacted.

The Republic was but just recovering from an exhausting war, which loaded it with a national debt approaching $3,000,000,000. There were also State, county, city, and town debts aggregating many more thousands of millions, with railroad and other corporate bonds and debts aggregating yet other thousands of millions and private debts of indefinite and unascertainable amount, represented largely by mortgages on real estate. This constituted an aggregate whose burden might naturally be presumed to be sufficient to tax all the resources of the people. Although some portion of those debts has been liquidated and the national bonds have been refunded at lower rates of interest, yet we all know that in this age all municipal and corporate debts, if not national debts, are practically perpetual. No sooner is one form of bond liquidated than another takes its place; no sooner is one public improvement completed than another is begun.

At the time silver was demonetized it might well have been supposed that a sufficiently large unearned increment had already been realized by the foreign and domestic holders of United States bonds. The greater portion of the debt of the Government was, when incurred, made payable simply in "lawful money"—the interest alone being payable in coin. Yet in March, 1869, the bond-holders secured the passage of an act of Congress, entitled "An act to strengthen the public credit," containing a pledge to pay in coin or its equivalent not merely the interest, but the principal of all national obligations not specially provided to be paid otherwise.

THE COURSE OF THE CREDITORS.

And again, when in 1870 Congress was about to provide for a refunding of the public debt, these clamorous creditors, not satisfied with having got the bonds at rates much below their face value, and not satisfied with the pledge to pay in coin—a pledge made long after the contract was made and the debt incurred—insisted that not only should the new bonds be payable in coin, but in order to guard against any possible interpretation which might work to their detriment they did what has rarely been done in the history of monetary legislation, insisted that even the very *standard* of that coin should be fixed and nominated in the bond. They were willing to take no chances. They were not willing to place confidence in the sense of equity and fair dealing of the people of the United States. They held before Congress the covert threat that if the new issue of bonds did not provide for payment in "coin," instead of "lawful money," and did not prescribe the precise standard of coin in which they were to be payable, it would be difficult if not impossible to place the bonds on the market.

So, by the refunding act of July 14, 1870, Congress provided for the payment in "coin of the present standard value," that is to say, in either gold dollars of 25.8 grains of gold, nine-tenths fine, or in silver dollars of 412½ grains of silver, nine-tentus fine, at the option of the United States. But even this extreme advantage to the creditors over payment in "lawful money" of the United States, in which the bonds were bought, and in which they were legally payable, was insufficient. All but the most ingenious would imagine that having thus provided for payment in coin then bearing a considerable premium over the current money of the Republic, and having the very standard of that coin fixed in the act, the highest point of vantage had been reached. One device, however, and only one, remained by which the money of the payment could be still further increased in value, and this device did not escape the watchful eye or cunning hand of the public creditors.

They clearly saw that if by legislative enactment they could secure the rejection of one of the money-metals they would succeed in enormously increasing the value of the metal retained. This they accomplished by the demonetization of silver, and thus by striking down one-half the automatic money of the world and devolving the money function exclusively on the other half, added thousands of millions of dollars to the burden of the debt.

THE PRETENSE TO "STRENGTHEN THE PUBLIC CREDIT."

It will be observed that this anxiety to strengthen the public credit was evinced by the bondholders *after* and not before the bonds were in their possession. No anxiety for the public credit was manifested by them at a time when the Government might be able to reap advantage from it. The Government having parted

JONES

2S

with the bonds at a heavy discount, their selling price in the market became a matter of no direct pecuniary importance to the people of the United States.

The "strengthening of the public credit" that was to be effected by the act of March 16, 1869, consisted of a rise in the price of the bonds for the benefit of the holder, at a time when they were no longer the property of the Government but of private individuals. The real effect of the act, therefore, was not in any way to benefit the Government but greatly to enrich, by an increment unearned and unbargained for, a few men who had already been greatly enriched by their dealings with the United States. The title of the act should have read "An act to strenghten the bank account and credit of the holders of United States bonds."

The excuse and apology for the act was that by its passage the refunding process then contemplated, and afterward provided for by the refunding act of 1870 might be rendered more certain of success; but if any advantage accrued from that cause, it was lost, and much more with it, by the increase which the act of 1869 effected in the burden of the bonded obligation, by pledging the nation to a payment in a medium much more valuable than the medium provided for in the contract. And, again, in 1873 when all the bonds provided for by the refunding act of 1870 had been sold and had passed out of the hands of the Government, another act was passed, intended by the money-lenders again to strengthen the public credit, and again to the disadvantage of the people and to the exclusive and enormous advantage of the bondholders. It bore the innocent title of "An act revising and amending the laws relative to the mints, assay offices, and coinage of the United States." This act, bearing on its face no suggestion of any change more serious than that of regulating the petty details of mint management, has proved to be an act of momentous consequence to the people of this country. This is the act that demonetized the silver dollar, which it did by merely omitting that coin from the enumeration of the coins of the United States.

DEMONETIZATION WHOLLY UNJUSTIFIABLE.

Among all the explanations that have been made to account for that demonetization by a Congress of the United States, I have never heard any reason advanced which constituted a justification for it. To my mind, in view of all the circumstances—in the face of the herculean difficulties by which the nation was surrounded, in the face of the sacrifices which our citizens had made to preserve he Republic, and in the face of all that had already been done by an over-generous people, proud of their national strength, and jealous of their national honor, to satisfy the rapacious demands of the money-lenders—in view, I say, of all these facts, the demonetization of silver by the United States must be regarded as one of those historic blunders that are worse than crimes. It was the child of Ignorance and Avarice, and is already the prolific parent of enforced idleness, poverty, and misery.

It is to undo as far as possible the effects of the blunder of 1873 that new legislation is now imperatively demanded by the people. While the past can not be recalled, the present is ours, and the pressing duty of to-day is to provide for the future. The demand comes from all sections of the country that a remedy for the depressed industrial conditions caused by the legislation of 1873, be applied at the earliest moment. And what better remedy could be applied than absolutely to reverse that legislation and to put the

JONES

monetary position of this country back to exactly where it was when that wrong was committed?

Some twelve years ago an attempt was made to apply a remedy, but the attempt was only partially successful. Instead of resulting in free coinage, it resulted in the passage of the bill which authorized the coinage of not less than two nor more than four million dollars' worth of silver per month. On that occasion a financial debate of great interest and importance was had in this Chamber and in the other House of Congress. The proposition to remonetize silver or to increase the silver coinage was vigorously opposed, but the arguments then presented by the advocates of remonetization never have been, and never can be, refuted.

In fact, but rarely has there been any attempt made to answer those arguments. Puerile attempts at wit, and diatribes of abuse are all that the silver men have heard in sixteen years in answer to the contentions they have made in favor of the remonetization of silver,

EDUCATIONAL EFFECT OF DISCUSSION.

With that debate, Mr. President, long pending and eagerly maintained on both sides, there began in this country an educational movement among the masses, that is destined to have far-reaching consequence. The public attention was fastened, as it had never been fastened before, on the subject of money, and on the forces which govern its value, and up to this time that attention has never flagged. As a result we find the great body of our people to-day—the farmers and artisans of the country—after years of reflection and discussion in their lyceums and trade organizations, adopting to a large extent the views then presented by the advocates of an increased money volume—views which at the time were contemptuously derided by the advocates of contraction and of gold.

The cry for relief appropriately now comes from the farmers, the artisans, and the laboring classes, as well as from the young, the enterprising, the thoughtful, of all classes, who have not inherited wealth, but are hewing out for themselves the rugged path to success. It is they who have had to bear the exactious of the system which has prevailed. It is from the proceeds of their labor that the extortious have been paid. If objection be made that the character of relief proposed is not indorsed in financial circles, or by the literary guild or professional political economists that surround them, the sufficient reply is that the world can not wait for the correction of abuses by those who are profiting by them. In the nature of things, all movements for reform must be initiated by those who can not lose by the installation of justice.

But there are others besides the laboring masses who are working in the cause of humanity. There are noble, unselfish, and altruistic men in all the countries of civilization, who see the wrong and are indefatigable in their efforts to set it right.

I will read a cable dispatch recently addressed to me by Mr. Henry H. Gibbs, formerly governor of the Bank of England, and now president of the Bimetallic League of Great Britain:

LONDON, May 6.—The friends of silver deeply regret the death of Senator Beck, whose services in the cause of monetary reform are most warmly appreciated on this side of the Atlantic. The bimetallist party of the United Kingdom, now including over one hundred members of the House of Commons, attach the greatest value to the debate about to commence in your illustrious chamber. We fully recognize not only that the support afforded to silver by your legislation during the last twelve years has helped to protect the industrial world from an acute monetary crisis, but also that the debates in Congress have served more than all else to educate our people to recognition of the important issues involved. We believe

JONES

also that the increase and coinage of silver contemplated by Congress will restore, wholly or considerably, your coinage rates, and will thus make international settlement of this complex question comparatively easy. We anticipate further and with much confidence, that the advance in the price of silver which must follow your action will stimulate both the export and the other trades of your country, and, while tending to the prosperity of your agricultural classes, will also assist the manufacturing industries of the United Kingdom and the whole body of our wage-earners.

Mr. Moreton Frewen, of London, an able writer on economic subjects, whose recent work on the "The Economic Crisis" I commend to the careful perusal of Senators, says:

It may, indeed, be affirmed, without fear of contradiction, that legislation arranged in the interest of a certain class, first by Lord Liverpool in this country, and again by Sir Robert Peel at the instigation of Mr. Jones Loyd and other wealthy bankers, which was supplemented recently by simultaneous anti-silver legislation in Berlin and Washington at the instance of the great financial houses—this legislation has about doubled the burden of all national debts by an artificial enhancement of the value of money.

The fall of all prices induced by this cause has been on such a scale that while in twenty years the National debt of the United States quoted in dollars has been reduced by nearly two-thirds, yet the value of the remaining one-third, measured in wheat, in bar iron, or bales of cotton, is considerably greater—is a greater demand draft on the labor and industry of the nation than was the whole debt at the time it was contracted. The aggravation of the burdens of taxation induced by this so-called "appreciation of gold," which is no natural appreciation, but has been brought about by class legislation to increase the value of the gold which is in a few hands, requires but to be explained to an enfranchised democracy, which will know how to protect itself against further attempts to contract the currency and to force down prices to the confusion of every existing contract.

Of all classes of middle-men, bankers have been by far the most successful in intercepting and appropriating an undue share of produced wealth. While the modern system of banking and credit may be said to be even yet in its infancy, that portion of the assets of the community which is to-day in the strong boxes of the bankers would, if declared, be an astounding revelation of the recent profits of this particular business; and not only has the business itself become a most profitable monopoly, but its interests in a very few hands are diametrically opposed to the general interests of the majority. By legislation intended to contract the currency and force down all prices, including wages, the price paid for labor, the money owner has been able to increase the purchase power of his sovereign or dollar by the direct diminution of the price of every kind of property measured in money.

UNFULFILLED PROPHECIES.

During the debate on the limited coinage bill, not content with abuse of the advocates of the measure; with flimsy criticism of it and specious arguments against it, its opponents in and out of Congress indulged in divers prophecies and predictions. They pictured forth the lamentable results that would follow its passage, and the direful consequences that would ensue from an increase of the circulating medium of the country. Among the results confidently predicted were the following: that the silver would not circulate at all, and again that it would circulate to the exclusion of gold, which metal, we were informed, would flow out of this country with a velocity and in a volume heretofore unknown; that we should be unable to redeem our paper money in gold; that we should be precipitated into a silver vortex; that an inflation of the currency would follow, which would ruinously raise prices of all commodities and that this inflation would result in an unprecedented contraction. We were charged with forcing upon the public creditors a dollar worth only ninety cents. We were warned that the passage of the bill would indefinitely postpone the refunding of the public debt, and would lower the price and impair the value of our national securities. It was charged that we were setting on foot a new and irrepressible conflict between two great sections of the country—the East and and the West. We were charged with uttering a debased coin; with

JONES

lowering the standard of American credit; with tarnishing the integrity and honor of our country before foreign nations, and with unprecedented moral turpitude in setting an example of flagrant and shameless national dishonesty.

The men of the far West, and of the Pacific slope especially, were the particular targets of this abuse. They were denounced by some as "lunatics," by others as dangerous and unworthy demagogues, because, as was charged, their constituents, if not themselves, were directly interested in the restoration of the ancient right of silver to full recognition as one of the money metals. For their benefit resort was had to every epithet which the English language afforded. In holding them up to public scorn the rich and varied vocabulary of odium and opprobrium was exhausted.

These prophecies of disaster were united in by the professors of political economy in all the Eastern colleges, by the President of the United States, by the Secretary of the Treasury, by the leading American newspapers, by the principal public men and journals of Great Britain, if not of all Europe; and, of course, by all bankers, money-lenders, and professional financiers the world over.

And now, Mr. President, how many of all those alarming prognostications by all these distinguished prophets have been fulfilled? Not one! On the contrary, it is not too much to say that the public credit of the United States is to-day the highest in the world. It does not stand merely in line with that of other first-rate powers; it stands at the head. Our gold, silver, and paper money stand at a parity with each other. If a full measure of relief was not realized by the passage of that bill it is because the coinage of $4,000,000 a month was left optional with the Secretary of the Treasury, instead of being made mandatory on him.

But it is hardly necessary to assert that the predicted inflation of prices has not been observed as a consequence of the coinage of $2,000,-000 a month. While the issuance of that amount has not, with our rapidly increasing population and wealth, been sufficient to arrest the downward tendency of prices, it has undoubtedly prevented them from falling much lower. Without that coinage, we should have had industrial depression, chronic and somber, with consequences of untold disaster.

But the result which gave most apprehension to those who advocated the gold standard, the evil which they regarded as on the whole the most threatening and direful of all the evils that were to result from even so small an increase in the money volume as that bill provided for, was the outflow of gold. They ridiculously under-estimated the tremendous money-absorbing power of this great country. And as if to emphasize to all the world the complete absurdity of their alleged fears—this apprehension has been conspicuously and notoriously set at naught by the constant inflow of gold. On the 30th of June, 1878, the amount of gold coin and bullion in the Treasury and in monetary circulation in this country is officially reported to have been $213,199,977, and this amount is probably much over-estimated. On November 1, 1889, we had more than three times as much—the amount of gold in circulation and in the Treasury being reported as $689,000,000.

"Experience," says Dr. Johnson, "is the great test of truth, and is perpetually contradicting the theories of men," and the last experience, Mr. President, is the best.

If the professors of political economy, the Eastern newspaper editors, and the professional financiers were then so seriously mistaken

JONES

• ought they not to be a little modest now in making predictions, especially in renewing predictions that have been already discredited ? They can not point to a single instance in which their prophesy has not been falsified by the event. So humiliating a failure on the part of the professors, in a realm of which they boastfully claimed to be masters, so complete an overthrow of these "experts" by men who were ridiculed and derided as rural financiers and crazy theorists, ought to put the advocates of the gold standard on their guard against a like defeat on this occasion. They are pressed for reasons to account for the utter miscarriage of their prophecies. They are left without a shadow of consolation except that the coinage of $2,000,000 worth of silver bullion each month has not succeeded in placing silver at a par with gold. They affect to believe that the advocates of silver in 1878 expected that that metal, under the very limited demand of $2,000,000 a month, would be brought to a level with gold, which, owing to the demonetization of silver, had risen abnormally and ruinously in value.

No such belief was ever entertained or expressed. On the contrary it was repeatedly asserted by the advocates of silver that so long as the entire yield of gold from all the mines of the world (in 1878, $119,000,000) was invested with the full money function and had free access to all mints to be transmuted into coin, it could not be expected that the conferring of the legal-tender function upon a sum so comparatively trifling as one-fourth the yield of silver (the yield in 1878 being $99,000,000) would have the effect of placing it on a level with gold.

It is, however, a significant fact that every silver dollar that has been coined under that act is at a parity with gold, and will to-day buy as much of all the objects of human desire as will the gold dollar. Nay, more, silver bullion—disparaged and discredited as it is by being shorn of the money function, and denied access to the mints, instead of decreasing in purchasing power, has maintained so steady a relation to commodities that 412½ grains of uncoined silver will exchange for as much to-day as would the coined dollar, whether of silver or gold, in 1873, when the full money function attached equally to both metals. If this be true—and I shall presently demonstrate it beyond refutation—what an utter perversion of terms it is to say that silver has fallen in value!

WILL REMONETIZATION PLACE US ALONGSIDE INDIA.

We are solemnly warned that the full remonetization of silver in the United States would place us alongside India and the other barbarous countries of the world. This brilliant piece of reasoning is advanced with great confidence, and is intended to be conclusive of the argument against silver. But, Mr. President, India is no more barbarous now than it was in 1873—before our silver dollar was demonetized. India is no more barbarous now than it was in 1857, when Germany demonetized gold and placed herself "alongside" India. Neither is Germany any more civilized now than then. We did not at that time hear any complaint, either in the United States or Europe, that the use of silver as money placed any one nation more than any other in dangerous affiliation with the civilization of India. We have never heard it charged against France that its civilization was brought any nearer that of India by the immense quantity of silver money in France. Neither did we hear it charged against the United States up to 1873 that we were "alongside," or dangerously close to the barbarous nations by our use of silver as money.

JONES

Up to 1834 we had no metallic money other than silver in our circulation, and up to 1850 we had much more silver in circulation than gold. Were we "alongside" India then? Where were the wise and patriotic men of our country at those periods? History fails to record any protest on their part that we were placing ourselves "alongside" India or any other of the barbarous nations of the world by our use of silver and our recognition of its full money power. All the nations of the earth used silver and accorded it full recognition as money equally with gold up to 1819. Was all Christendom at that time "alongside" India? When, in that year, Great Britain sundered the silver link that from time immemorial had kept her "alongside" India and the other barbarous nations and, for selfish reasons of her own, arising from her position as a creditor of all other nations, decided to recognize gold only as money, was any evidence afforded of a sudden advance in the civilization of Great Britain? Was the emergence of that nation from the benumbing companionship of India and the other barbaric countries into the glittering and refulgent light of the gold dispensation signalized, as would be expected, by a corresponding improvement in the condition of the people?

On the contrary, the history of the time informs us that as a consequence of the passage of the bill by Parliament in 1819, compelling payments in gold, prices rapidly fell, cotton in particular sinking in the short space of three months to one-half its former level. Within six months all prices had fallen one-half, and showed no signs of improvement for the next three years. By reason of the contraction of the currency the industry of the nation was congealed, as is a flowing stream by the severity of an arctic winter. Alarm became universal; confidence and activity ceased. Bankruptcies increased in 1819 more than 50 per cent. over the number of the previous year. Meetings were held throughout England in which the people called on the government to devise some means of redressing the situation. So universal was the distress that the owners of land in England, who in 1819 numbered 160,000 were in seven years, by forced sales and foreclosure of mortgages on the smaller farms, reduced to 30,000, and one in every seven of the population lived on organized charity. All this was but a part of the price which the people of England paid for a policy imposed on them by the creditor classes among their own number. The condition of industry and disorganization of labor led to frequent and serious conflicts between the people and the military. They also led to commercial crises without number, and England, by demonetizing silver and thus ceasing to be "alongside" India, became the seat of panics, as Egypt had long been of the plague and India of the cholera.

As a contrast to this I will merely cite the change in the condition of India within the past seventeen years. When the Western world discarded silver as money and, as a consequence, India received a larger supply of it than ever before, that barbarous nation, as is universally admitted, made progress by leaps and bounds. No country on earth has in the same time made such advances in material prosperity and in all the elements that conduce to the comfort and happiness of a people. Notwithstanding the alleged debasement of silver, no sooner had its increased inflow into India begun than the industries of a vast continent were established and set in motion, and a substantial part of the activity and prosperity that were wont to pervade some of the industries of the United States has, by that

demonctization, been transferred to fields of wheat, and fields and factories of cotton 10,000 miles distant.
What really placed us alongside such barbarous countries as India was the demonetization of silver. It was by that demonetization that the people of Europe were enabled, with gold, to buy silver at 30 per cent. discount, which, when shipped to India and coined into rupees, would buy as much wheat as could ever have been bought with that coin. There has been no decrease whatever in the purchasing power of the rupee in India. This was equivalent to buying wheat at 30 per cent. below the price theretofore paid for it, and thus the farmers of the United States were by demonctization placed "alongside" the barbarous people of India. Their wheat had to compete in the European markets with the wheat of India, and it is this competition that placed them "alongside" India. The farmer of this country, therefore, by demonetization of silver, was compelled to compete with under-paid and half-starved ryots. And so it was that our cotton planters, by the demonctization of silver, were placed alongside the barbarous people of India. It is this degrading competition that places a highly civilized people alongside a barbarous one.

The advocates of the single gold standard deem even silver money much better than greenbacks. Does it then follow that when greenbacks were our only money—good enough money to carry the nation through the greatest war in all history—we were "alongside" or underneath the barbarous nations of the world? It is not the form, or the material of a nation's money that fixes its status relatively to other nations. That is accomplished by the vitality, the energy, the intellectuality and effective force of its people. The United States can never be placed "alongside" any barbarous nation, except by compelling our people to compete with barbarous peoples—compelling them to sell the products of American labor at prices regulated by the cost of labor and manner of living in barbarous countries. As well might it be said that we are alongside the barbarous people of India because we continue to produce wheat and cotton.

The distinguishing feature of all barbarous nations is the squalor of their working classes. The reward of their hard toil is barely enough to maintain animal existence. A civilized people are placed alongside a barbarous one when, in their means of livelihood, the foundation of their civilization, they are made to compete with the barbarians. That was the result accomplished for the farmers and planters of the United States when silver was demonetized.

CREDITORS AND DEBTORS.—A COMPARISON OF MOTIVES.

All movements for the increase of the monetary circulation are ascribed by the money-lenders and creditor classes to the unworthy desire on the part of the debtors to escape their just obligations. But if motives are to be brought in question, the rule should work both ways. No note is taken of the motive of the creditor classes in securing a contraction of the circulation. Whatever the apparent purpose of contraction, and however specious the arguments advanced in its justification, the real object has always been to increase the purchasing power of money. In all countries, and throughout all time, it is the cupidity of the creditor classes and annuitants, and their desire to increase the value of the money unit that has brought about a shrinkage in the money volume. Unlike the great masses of the people, who were ignorant of the effects to be naturally expected from such a shrinkage, the annuitants and moneyed men very well understood that the value of every pound or dollar depended on the number of pounds or dollars that were in circulation; the larger the total number out, the smaller the purchasing power of each; the smaller the total number out, the greater the purchasing power of each.

Loaners of capital are not usually those who entertain further hope of personal achievement. When men realize fortunes it is rarely that they conserve the faculty of initiative; they find no special delight in novelty; they look so carefully to security in the use of money that the spirit of adventure is restrained. The realization of a fortune is usually the labor of a life-time, and few men who reach the goal care to retrace their steps to enter again upon a struggle that demands all the strength, the momentum, and the intrepidity of youth. Men of assured incomes therefore are disposed to take their ease, and society must look, for its material progress and development, to those who have a career to make, with the ambition and the power to make it.

It is a remarkable circumstance, Mr. President, that throughout the entire range of economic discussion in gold-standard circles, it seems to be taken for granted that a change in the value of the money unit is a matter of no significance, and imports no mischief to society, so long as the change is in one direction. Who has ever heard from an Eastern journal any complaint against a contraction of our money volume; any admonition that in a shrinking volume of money lurk evils of the utmost magnitude? On the other hand we have been treated to lengthy homilies on the evils of "inflation," whenever the slightest prospect presented itself of a decrease in the value of money—not with the view of giving the debtor an advantage over the lender of money, but of preventing the unconscionable injustice of a further increasing value in the dollars which the debtor contracted to pay. Loud and resounding protests have been entered against the "dishonesty" of making payments in "depreciated dollars." The debtors are characterized as dishonest for desiring to keep money at a steady and unwavering value. If that object could be secured, it would undoubtedly be to the interest of the debtor, and could not possibly work any injustice to the creditor. It would simply assure to both debtor and creditor the exact measure for which they bargained. It would enable the debtor to pay his debt with exactly the amount of sacrifice to which, on the making of the debt, he undertook to submit, in order to pay it.

WHO ARE THE DEBTORS?

In all discussions of the subject the creditors attempt to brush aside the equities involved by sneering at the debtors. But, Mr. President, debt is the distinguishing characteristic of modern society. It is through debt that the marvelous developments of nineteenth century civilization have been effected. Who are the debtors in this country? Who are the borrowers of money? The men of enterprise, of energy, of skill, the men of industry, of foresight, of calculation, of daring. In the ranks of the debtors will be found a large preponderance of the constructive energy of every country. The debtors are the upbuilders of the national wealth and prosperity; they are the men of initiative, the men who conceive plans and set on foot enterprises. They are those who by borrowing money enrich the community. They are the dynamic force among the people. They are the busy, restless, moving throng whom you find in all walks of life in this country—the active, the vigorous, the strong, the undaunted.

These men are sustained in their efforts by the hope and belief that their labors will be crowned with success. Destroy that hope and

JONES

you take away from society the most powerful of all the incentives to material development; you place in the pathway of progress an obstacle which it is impossible to surmount.

The men of whom I have spoken are undoubtedly the first who are likely to be affected by a shrinkage in the volume of money.

The highest prosperity of a nation is attained only when all its people are employed in avocations suited to their individual aptitudes, and when a just money system insures an equitable distribution of the products of their industry. With our present complex civilization, in order that men may have constant employment, it is indispensable that work be planned and undertakings projected years in advance. Without an intelligent forecast of enterprises large numbers of workmen must periodically be relegated to idleness. Enterprises that take years to complete must be contracted for in advance, and payments provided for.

A constant but unperceived rise in the value of the dollar with which those payments must be made, baffles all plans, thwarts all calculation, and destroys all equities between debtor and creditor. If we can not intelligently regulate our money volume so as to maintain unchanging the value of the money unit, if we can not preserve our people from the blighting effects which an increase in the measuring power of the money unit entails upon all industry, to what purpose is our boasted civilization?

By the increase of that measuring power all hopes are disappointed, all purposes baffled, all efforts thwarted, all calculations defied. This subtle enlargement in the measuring power of the unit of money (the dollar) affects every class of the working community. Like a poisonous drug in the human body, it permeates every vein, every artery, every fiber and filament of the industrial structure. The debtor is fighting for his life against an enemy he does not see, against an influence he does not understand. For, while his calculations were well and intelligently made, and the amount of his debts and the terms of his contracts remain the same, the weight of all his obligations has been increased by an insidious increase in the value of the money unit.

EFFECTS OF A SHRINKING VOLUME OF MONEY.

As to the benumbing consequences following a shrinkage in the volume of money, the testimony of history is briefly reviewed in the report of the Monetary Commission to which I have already referred, and from which I read the following:

At the Christian era the metallic money of the Roman Empire amounted to $1,800,000,000. By the end of the fifteenth century it had shrunk to less than $200,000,000. During this period a most extraordinary and baleful change took place in the condition of the world. Population dwindled and commerce, arts, wealth, and freedom all disappeared. The people were reduced by poverty and misery to the most degraded conditions of serfdom and slavery. The disintegration of society was almost complete. The conditions of life were so hard that individual selfishness was the only thing consistent with the instinct of self preservation. All public spirit, all generous emotions, all the noble aspirations of man shriveled and disappeared as the volume of money shrunk and as prices fell.

History records no such disastrous transition as that from the Roman Empire to the Dark Ages. Various explanations have been given of this entire breaking down of the framework of society, but it was certainly coincident with a shrinkage in the volume of money, which was also without historical parallel. The crumbling of institutions kept even step and pace with the shrinkage in the stock of money and the falling of prices. All other attendant circumstances than these last have occurred in other historical periods unaccompanied and unfollowed by any such mighty disasters. It is a suggestive coincidence that the first glimmer of light only came with the invention of bills of exchange and paper substitutes, through which the scanty stock of the precious metals was increased in efficiency. But not less than the energizing influence of Potosi and all the argosies of treasure from the New World were needed to arouse the Old World from its comatose sleep, to quicken the torpid limbs of industry, and to plume the leaden wings of commerce. It needed the heroic treatment of rising prices to enable society to reunite its shattered links, to shake off the shackles of fendalism, to relight and uplift the almost extinguished torch of civilization. That the disasters of the Dark Ages were caused by decreasing money and falling prices, and that the recovery therefrom and the comparative prosperity which followed the discovery of America were dne to an increasing supply of the precious metals and rising prices, will not seem surprising or unreasonable when the noble functions of money are considered. Money is the great instrument of association, the very fiber of social organism, the vitalizing force of industry, the protoplasm of civilization, and as essential to its existence as oxygen is to animal life. Without money civilization conld not have had a beginning; with a dininishing snpply it must languish, and, unless relieved, finally perish.

Symptoms of disasters similar to those which befell society during the Dark Ages were observable on every hand during the first half of this century. In 1809 the revolutionary troubles between Spain and her American colonies broke out. These troubles resulted in a great diminution in the production of the precions metals, which was quickly indicated by a fall in general prices. As already stated in this report, it is estimated that the pnrchasing power of the precious metals increased between 1809 and 1848 fully 145 per cent., or, in other words, that the general range of prices was 60 per cent. lower in 1848 than it was in 1809. During this period there was no general demonetization of either metal and no important flnctuation in the relative value of the metals, and the supply was sufficient to keep their stock good against losses by accident and abrasion. But it was insufficient to keep the stock up to the proper correspondence with the increasing demand of advancing populations.

The world has rarely passed through a more gloomy period than this one. Again do we find falling prices and misery and destitution inseparable companions. The poverty and distress of the industrial masses were intense and universal, and, since the discovery of the mines of America, without a parallel. In England the suffering of the people fonnd expression in demands npon Parliament for relief, in bread-riots, and in immense Chartist demonstrations. The military arm of the nation had to be strengthened to prevent the all-pervading discontent from ripening into open revolt. On the Continent the fires of revolution smoldered everywhere, and blazed out at many poiuts, threatening the overthrow of states and the subversion of social institutions.

Whenever and wherever the mutterings of discontent were hushed by the fear of increased standing armies, the foundations of society were honey-combed by powerful secret political associations. The cause at work to produce this state of things was so subtile, and its advance so silent, that the masses were entirely iguorant of its nature. They had come to regard money as an institution fixed and immovable in value, aud when the price of propprty and the wages of labor fell, they charged the fault, not to the money, but to the property and the employer. They were taught that the mischief was the result of overproduction. Never having observed that overproduction was complained of only when the money stock was decreasing, their prejudices were aroused against labor-saving machinery. They were angered at capital, because it either declined altogether to embark in industrial enteiprises or would only embark in them upon the condition of employing labor at the most scanty remuneration. They forgot that falling prices compelled capital to avoid such enterprises on any other condition, and for the most part to avoid them entirely. They did not comprehend that money in shrinking volnme was the prolifio parent of euforced idleness and poverty, and that falling prices divorced money-capital, from labor, but they none the less felt the paralyzing pressure of the shrinking metallic shroud that was closing around industry.

The increased yield of the Rnssian gold fields in 1846 gave some relief and served as a parachute to tho fall in prices, which might otherwise have resulted in a great catastrophe. But the enormons metallic supplies of California and Anstralia were all needed to give substantial and adequate relief. Great as these supplies were, their influence in raising prices was moderate and soon entirely arrested by the increasing populations and commerce which followed them. In the twenty-five years between 1850 and 1876 the money stock of the world was more than doubled, and yet at no time during this period was the general level of prices raised more than 18 per cent. above the general level in 1848.

A comparison of this effect of an increasing volnme of money after 1848 with the effect of a decreasing volume between 1809 and 1848 strikingly illustrates how largely different iu degree is the influence upon prices of an increasing or decreasing volume of money. The decrease of the yield of the mines since about 1865, while population and commerce have been advancing, has already prodnced unmistakable symptoms of the same general distrust, non-employment of labor, and political and social disquiet, which have characterized all former periods of shrinking money.

JONES

The time that has elapsed since that report was written has but served to verify and emphasize its statements.

THE FALL OF PRICES SINCE 1873.

It is a fact not disputed anywhere but universally admitted, that for many years past the prices of all articles entering into general consumption among the people have been steadily falling. It is obvious that the industrial conditions prevailing since 1873 are but a repetition of those above described as following 1809—with falling prices, constant unrest, and universal discontent.

The following table, compiled from figures published by the Bureau of Statistics of the Treasury Department, shows the average range of export prices of the articles named for each year since 1873:

Annual average export prices of commodities of domestic production for each year from 1873 to 1889, inclusive.

Year ending June, 30—	Corn per bushel.	Wheat per bushel.	Wheat flour per barrel.	Cotton (upland) per pound.	Leather per pound.	Illuminating oils, refined, per gallon.	Bacon and hams per pound.	Lard per pound.
	Dollars.	Dollars.	Dollars.	Cents.	Cents.	Cents.	Cents.	Cents.
1873	.618	1.312	7.565	18.8	25.3	23.5	8.8	9.2
1874	.719	1.428	7.144	15.4	25.2	17.3	9.0	9.4
1875	.848	1.124	5.968	15.0	26.0	14.1	11.4	18.8
1876	.672	1.242	6.216	12.9	26.2	14.0	12.1	13.3
1877	.587	1.160	6.484	11.8	23.9	21.1	10.8	10.9
1878	.562	1.338	6.358	11.1	21.8	14.4	8.7	8.8
1879	.471	1.008	5.252	9.9	20.4	10.8	6.9	7.0
1880	.543	1.245	5.878	11.5	23.3	8.6	6.7	7.4
1881	.552	1.114	5.663	11.4	22.6	10.3	8.2	9.3
1882	.668	1.185	6.149	11.4	20.9	9.1	9.9	11.6
1883	.684	1.127	5.955	10.8	21.1	8.8	11.2	11.9
1884	.611	1.066	5.568	10.5	20.6	9.2	10.2	9.5
1885	.540	.862	4.807	10.6	19.8	8.7	9.2	7.9
1886	.498	.870	4.699	9.9	19.9	8.7	7.5	6.9
1887	.479	.890	4.510	9.5	18.7	7.8	7.9	7.1
1888	.550	.853	4.579	9.8	17.3	7.9	8.6	7.7
1889	.474	.897	4.832	9.9	16.6	7.8	8.6	8.6

Year ending June 30—	Pork, salted, per pound.	Beef, salted, per pound.	Butter per pound.	Cheese per pound.	Eggs per dozen.	Starch per pound.	Sugar, refined, per pound.	Tobacco, leaf, per pound.
	Cents.	Cents.	Cents.	Cents.	Cents.	Cents.	Cents.	Cents.
1873	7.8	7.7	21.1	12.1	20.6	5.3	11.0	10.7
1874	8.2	8.2	25.0	13.1	22.1	5.7	10.5	9.6
1875	10.1	8.7	21.7	18.5	25.6	0.0	10.8	11.8
1876	10.6	8.7	21.0	12.6	28.0	5.4	10.7	10.4
1877	9.0	7.5	20.6	11.8	25.9	4.2	11.6	10.2
1878	6.8	7.7	18.0	11.4	15.8	4.7	10.2	8.7
1879	5.7	6.3	14.2	8.9	14.5	4.2	8.5	7.8
1880	6.1	6.4	17.1	9.5	16.5	4.3	9.0	7.7
1881	7.7	6.5	19.8	11.1	17.2	4.7	9.2	8.3
1882	9.0	8.5	19.3	11.0	19.2	4.8	8.7	8.5
1883	9.9	8.9	18.0	11.8	20.9	4.6	9.2	8.6
1884	7.9	7.6	18.2	10.3	21.2	4.5	7.1	9.1
1885	7.2	7.5	16.8	9.3	21.5	4.0	6.4	9.0
1886	5.9	6.0	15.6	8.3	18.3	4.1	6.7	7.8
1887	6.6	6.4	15.8	9.3	16.3	3.8	6.0	8.7
1888	7.4	5.3	18.3	9.9	12.0	3.5	6.8	8.3
1889	7.4	5.5	16.5	9.3	13.9	3.8	7.6	8.8

To show from another source the same general fact of the decline of prices, I quote from an article published in the New York Tribune early in 1886.

The New York Tribune is pretty good authority. These figures are undoubtedly from the calculations and from the pen of Mr. Grosvenor, of the editorial staff of that able journal, formerly editor and proprietor of the "Public," whose estimates of prices have, in my judgment, been more correctly made than those of any other statistician in the world. The article is as follows:

Quotations of about two hundred articles are compared since 1860, and the amount of money is ascertained which would purchase, at different dates, of these various articles, quantities corresponding as closely as possible to their ascertained consumption in 1880, the date of the last census. Among the articles compared are wheat, corn, oats, rye, barley, beans and pease, mess pork, bacon, ham, live hogs, lard, fresh beef, tallow, live sheep, poultry, butter, cheese, eggs, milk, hay, potatoes, turnips, cabbage, onions, apples, raisins, sugar, brown and crushed ; molasses, coffee, tea, tobacco, whisky, malt and hops, mackerel, codfish, salt, rice, nutmegs, cloves, pepper, cotton, print-cloths and standard sheeting, wool of different qualities, blankets, carpets, flannels, leather, boots, shoes, hides, silk, India rubber, iron (pig and bar), nails, steel rails, coal, oil (crude and refined), tin and tin plates, copper, lead, hemp, lumber, spruce and pine, oak, ash, walnut, and white wood, lath, brick, lime, turpentine, linseed oil, soap, glass, paper, white lead, and twelve other kinds of paints, fertilizers, and over fifty kinds of drugs and chemicals.

*   *   *   *   *   *

Cost of products at different dates.

Dates.	Cost in currency.	Price of gold.	Cost in gold.
1860, May 1	$100.00	$100.00	$100.00
1865, November 1	174.77	145.87	119.81
1866, May 1	157.60	125.12	126.04
1866, November 1	170.31	146.25	117.82
1871, November 1	122.03	112.00	108.95
1872, May 1	137.13	112.50	121.81
1873, November 1	115.14	108.50	106.01
1874, May 1	122.77	112.87	108.77
1875, January 1	113.01	112.37	100.37
1876, October 1	97.30	110.00	88.45
1877, May 1	99.29	106.75	93.01
1878, May 1	82.09	100.37	81.81
1878, October 18	77.94	100.37	77.63
1879, November 1	93.48		
1860, January 1	103.42		
1881, January 1	95.98		
1882, May 16	100.59		
1883, March 13	97.82		
1883, November 1	88.71		
1884, January 1	88.37		
1884, November 21	78.47		
1885, January 1	79.66		
1885, May 9	80.22		
1885, August 22	74.56		
1885, November 1	75.35		
1885, Close*	78.53		

It is not only clear from this comparison that the prices of 1885 have been the lowest in our history for twenty-five years, but that there has been a general tendency toward lower prices. From 1866 to 1871, and again from 1872 until 1885, prices fell quite steadily. Indeed, had not the short crop of 1881 caused a temporary advance in the spring of 1882, the range of January, 1880, would have been the highest of the later period, and it might have been said that the present era of declining prices had continued with little intermission for six years. None will fail to observe how swift and sharp the advances have been—about 12 per cent. from November, 1871, to May, 1872, and 25½ per cent. from October, 1878, to January, 1880.

JONES

But these spasmodic advances, by which the general tendency downward is interrupted, only serve to make it more clear that prices have been tending irresistibly toward a lower level than that of 1860, not only during the period of paper depreciation, but since gold has been the measure of value.

In order to show that the United States are not alone in their complaint of falling prices, but that the complaint is universal, and in order that we may have before us a broad view of the field of general prices, I submit a table showing the relation to each other of the range of prices from 1809 to 1849, by decades, based on the prices of fifty leading articles of commerce, prepared by the distinguished Professor Jevons and published in the London Economist for May 8, 1869.

Taking the range of prices of 1849 as a datum line (the range for that year being the lowest of the century) Mr. Jevons works backward to 1809, when the revolt of the South American colonies against the authority of Spain shut off at a blow the supplies of the precious metals, and set on foot a money famine from which the world knew no relief till the discovery of the mines of California and Australia.

Professor Jevons's figures are as follows, the prices of 1849 being represented by 100:

Relation of prices, 1809 to 1849, by decades, those for 1849 being rated at 100.

1809	245
1819	175
1829	124
1839	144
1849	100

From these figures it will be observed that the fall from 1809 to 1849, a period of forty years, was as 245 to 100, or 59 per cent.

By the next table which I submit, that of Dr. Soetbeer, it will be seen that the general range of prices rose gradually from 1849 to 1873, in the last of which years the figures bore to those of 1849 the relation of 138 to 100. It has never been denied that this rise was due to the increase in the world's money supply by the yield of the precious metals from the mines of California and Australia, the effects of which, however, as will be seen by the table, were not felt on prices till 1853—five years after John Marshall's discovery of the yellow metal in the tail-race at Sutter's mills. Yet, because it interferes with the pecuniary interests of a large and influential class, it is vehemently denied that the fall of prices since 1873 is due to a decrease in the volume of the money caused by the demonetization of silver in that year throughout the western world.

From and after that year, as will be perceived by an examination of the figures; in other words, from the year when one-half the world's money supply was deprived of the money function, we find an almost uninterrupted decline of prices. The figures of 1873 and 1885 will be seen to bear to one another the relation of 138 to 108, or a fall of 22 per cent. In twelve years. Should the fall continue at that rate without interruption—and there is no reason apparent why it should not, we shall in forty years have witnessed a decline of 72 per cent. in the general range of prices—a decline considerably greater than that from 1809 to 1849. And these are not the figures of bimetallists or silver "theorists," but of pronounced advocates of the single standard of gold. Where, I would inquire, is the fall of prices to stop?

Dr. Soetbeer's table represents the general average price of one-hundred leading articles of commerce each year for a period of nearly forty years. He takes as a basis the general range of gold prices pre-

JONES

vailing between 1847 and 1850, and calling that range 100, shows the
relative standing toward it of the general range of prices for subsequent years, up to 1835.

*Relation of prices by years from 1849 to 1885, the general range of
prices of 1849 being rated at 100.*

1849	100.00	1869	123.38
1851	100.21	1870	122.87
1852	101.69	1871	127.03
1853	113.69	1872	135.62
1854	121.25		
1855	124.23	1873	138.28
1856	123.27		
1857	130.11	1874	136.20
1858	113.52	1875	120.85
1859	116.34	1876	128.33
1860	120.98	1877	127.70
1861	118.10	1878	120.60
1862	122.65	1879	117.10
1863	125.49	1880	121.89
1864	129.28	1881	121.07
1865	122.64	1882	122.14
1866	125.85	1883	122.24
1867	124.44	1884	114.25
1868	121.99	1885	108.27

Mr. Sauerbeck, also an advocate of the gold standard, and whose
work has the approval of the Statistical Society, takes as a datum
line the prices ruling from 1867 to 1870. Rating those at 100 he
finds that by 1873 prices had risen to 111, by 1886 they had fallen to
69, and by September, 1887, to 63.7. He declares the average prices
for the first nine months of 1887 to have been the lowest reached for
a hundred years.

BOTH GOLD AND SILVER VARIABLE IN VALUE.

The fact that the metals have separated considerably since 1873,
and that silver bullion now sells at less than par value of $1.29 per
ounce, is taken to signify that silver has fallen—not that gold has
risen. This proceeds from the assumption that whenever a change
takes place in the relation between gold and any other article the
change must necessarily be in the other article. This assumption,
in turn, is based on the absurd idea that calling gold a "standard"
will insure it against change.

Among political economists it is a well-recognized principle that
neither gold or silver is exempt from the universal application of
the law of supply and demand. That law governs gold and silver,
not only as commodities, but as money, and governs as well all
other kinds of money that may be used. And while the advocate of
the single gold standard is at all times ready to concede the truth of
this assertion as to silver, he is confident that it does not and can
not apply to gold; that the economic law which makes supply and
demand a regulator of value is suspended as to gold.

That a metallic money, whether of gold or silver, is very far from
being stable is admitted by innumerable authorities, of whom I will
cite only a few.

Dr. Adam Smith, in his "Wealth of Nations," book 1, chapter 5,
says:

Gold and silver, like every other commodity, vary in their value. The discovery of the abundant mines of America reduced in the sixteenth century the
value of gold and silver in Europe to about a third of what it had been before.
This revolution in their value, though perhaps the greatest, is by no means the
only one of which history gives some account.

JONES

And again:

Increase the scarcity of gold to a certain degree and the smallest bit of it may be more precious than a diamond.

John Locke, "Considerations, etc., in relation to money" (published in 1691), says:

The greater scarcity of money enhances its price and increases the scramble; there being nothing that does supply the want of it; the lessening of its quaniity, therefore, always increases its price and makes an equal portion of it exchange for a greater of any other thing.

Prof. Francis A. Walker, "Money," etc., page 210, says:

Gold and silver do, over long periods, undergo great changes of value and become in a high degree deceptive as a measure of the obligation of the debtor of the claim of the creditor. Thus Prof-essor Jevons estimates that the value of gold fell between 1789 and 1809, 46 per cent., that from 1809 to 1819 it rose 145 per cent, while in twenty years after 1849 it fell again at least 20 per cent.

Jevons, "Money and Exchange," chapter 6, says:

In respect to steadiness of value the metals are probably less satisfactory, regarded as a standard of value, than many other commodities, such as corn.

And again, in chapter 24 of the same work, he says:

We are too much accustomed to look upon the value of gold as a fixed datum line in commerce; but in reality it is a very variable thing.

Sir Archibald Alison (England, in 1815 and 1845), says:

The coining of gold and silver, which is universal in all civilized nations, and affixing to them one definite and permanent value by authority of law, has no effect whatever in preventing the fluctuations in the real value of the current coin of the realm.

Professor Langhlin, of Harvard, in his work on Political Economy (page 72), says:

It is quite evident that the name dollar does not always have the same value, although people often think it does. We get into the habit of using names without thinking what they really mean. The 23.22 grains in a gold dollar may be exchanged sometimes for more, sometimes for less, of other commodities. When it is exchanged for less. Its value has fallen relatively to all other commodities, and, even if the name dollar remains the same, its value has fallen. One must then offer more dollars than before for the same commodities. That is, when money falls in value, prices rise; when money rises in value, prices fall.

Now, we shall say a few words in regard to another function, a means of paying long contracts, or debts which run over a long term of years.

Suppose that I loaned you in 18-0, $1,000 for twenty years. In that year the $1,000 bought a certain quantity of corn, wheat, sugar, salt, wood, hats, and shoes. In 1900, when you are to pay me back the $1,000 in money, if prices have changed, you may give me back the same amount of money, but you will not return to me the same purchasing power over other things. If for some reason prices have fallen between 1880 and 1900, it will take less money to buy the same quantity as before of corn, wheat, etc. If so, the $1,000 you return me in 1900 will be of more value than the $1,000 I gave you, and it would be unjust to oblige you to give me more than you borrowed. If, on the other hand, prices have risen, then the $1,000 in money would buy me less than before, so that I should lose. * * * Hence, the value of money (gold or silver) does not remain the same for any length of time; and the precious metals, while they are very satisfactory for exchanges which do not take very long to complete, can not serve as a proper measure of value during a long term of years.

Ricardo, the greatest authority on the gold standard, the financial writer, more highly regarded throughout the world than any other that has ever appeared in Great Britain, whose logical utterances have never failed to attract the attention of mankind, stated the true condition of things in 1810, and advocated the true policy for Great Britain.

JONES

In his "Proposals for an Economical and Secure Currency," Ricardo makes the following statement, which I commend to the careful attention of the advocates of the single gold standard:

While a standard is used, we are subject to only such a variation in the value of money as the standard itself is subject to; but against such variation there is no possible remedy, and late events have proved that, during periods of war, when gold and silver are used for the payment of large armies distant from home, those variations are much more considerable than has been generally allowed. This admission only proves that gold and silver are not so good a standard as they have been hitherto supposed—that they are themselves subject to greater variations than it is desirable a standard should be subject to. They are, however, the best with which we are acquainted.

If any other commodity less variable could be found, it might very properly be adopted as the future standard of our money, provided it had all the other qualities which fitted it for that purpose; but while these metals are the standard the currency should conform in value to them, and whenever it does not, and the market price of bullion is above the mint price, the currency is depreciated. This proposition is unanswered and is unanswerable. Much inconvenience arises from using two metals as a standard of our money; and it has long been a disputed point whether gold or silver should by law be made the principal or sole standard of money. In favor of gold it may be said, that its greater value under a small bulk eminently qualifies for a standard in an opulent country.

And I may here remark that it requires an opulent country to maintain the single gold standard, and the country does maintain it at very great expense. I do not wonder that he thought an opulent country, a creditor country, the only one that ought to adopt it, for no other country can afford to adopt it. But, like many people who in attempting to improve their condition in society attempt luxuries and extravagances which they can not maintain and which force them back into the ranks from which they came, so nations in attempting to establish the gold standard may find themselves reduced from opulence to poverty.

Ricardo continues:

But this very quality subjects to greater variations of value during periods of war or extensive commercial discredit, when it is often collected and hoarded, and may be urged as an argument against its use. The only objection to the use of silver as the standard is its bulk, which renders it unfit for the large payments required in a wealthy country; but this objection is entirely removed by the substituting of paper money as the general circulation medium of the country. Silver, too, is much more steady in its value in consequence of its demand and supply being more regular; and, as all foreign countries regulate the value of their money by the value of silver, there can be no doubt that on the whole silver is preferable to gold as a standard, and should be permanently adopted for that purpose.

Innumerable additional citations from authors of repute could be adduced to fortify this position.

It will thus be seen that the fluctuations in the value or purchasing power of both gold and silver have always been admitted by scientific writers. They were so well understood three centuries ago that in Queen Elizabeth's reign (1576) the British Parliament directed that the rents reserved in the long leases of certain college lands should be payable, not in money, but in wheat. And at various times during the past seventy years propositions have been formulated to substitute for gold and silver as a standard of value for deferred payments, a tabular statement of the prices of the principal articles of commerce, to be made by official authority and published from time to time, by the average of which the fluctuations of gold could be ascertained and proper allowance made for them in the settlement of time transactions. Professor Jevons, Prof. Francis A. Walker, and other political economists of note have expressed approval of such a tabular standard for long-time contracts, as securing greater equity than would gold as a measure of values. Those who now assert that silver has fallen and that gold has not

JONES

risen in value arrive at this conclusion by a very safe process of reasoning. First, to show that silver has fallen they measure it by gold alone, without reference to the general range of prices; and then to prove that gold has not risen they make it the measure of itself. An increase or decrease of the value of either can not be ascertained by reference to the other, and certainly not by constituting either of them a standard by which to judge itself. It would of course be forever impossible to show any change in the value of gold or silver, or of anything else, measuring it by itself. It is only by looking at the relations which both metals bear respectively to a considerable range of commodities generally dealt in as well as to each other, that it can be ascertained with certainty what has happened.

Not only upon consideration of all the facts I have given, but upon the logic of the situation, it must be obvious that gold has risen and will continue to rise in value as long as its volume decreases and the demand for it increases. Since 1860, when gold constituted 77 per cent. of the combined yield of the two metals, it has diminished not only in relative proportion to the yield of silver, but it has diminished absolutely. For the five years ending with 1860 the yield of gold throughout the world was $137,000,000 a year; for the five years ending 1889 the yield was but $110,000,000 a year. If, as claimed by the advocates of the single gold standard, an increase in the yield of silver decreases the value of silver, by what system of logic can they deny that a decrease in the supply of gold increases the value of gold?

In a late issue of the London Economist, that of April 26, 1890, I find an editorial article relating to the recent discussion on bimetallism in the British House of Commons. That article comments somewhat sharply on Mr. Smith's assertion that "a conspiracy had been formed among the financial class in Europe and America to get rid of silver as full-valued money in order to increase the value of gold, in which their revenues are paid." In the course of his comments the editor, by "confession and avoidance," admits our whole contention as to the rise of gold and the fall, as a natural consequence, of the prices of commodities. He says:

It may not be amiss, however, to point out that the increase in the exchangeable value of gold has been by no means such a gain to the financial class as he in common with many others suppose; for advantage has been very largely taken of it to cut down the return upon the capital which the financial classes have invested. It has favored debt conversion schemes, and it has been one of the influences that have caused the rate of interest in general to decline so decidedly, that, all round, the yield of investments is now very appreciably lower than it was fifteen years ago. The idea that the creditor class have realized unmixed gains and the debtor class have suffered unmitigated losses by the alteration in the purchasing power of gold is thus altogether fallacious. There has in their case, as in all others, been a species of compulsory give and take. Each has gained and each has lost something, and now that the process of readjustment has been carried so far it would be unwise to the last degree to unsettle everything again by such legislation as the bimetallists propose.

The editor of the Economist is to be commended for at least one thing. He does not quibble as to the most important point in the bimetallic controversy. He frankly admits that gold has risen, and does not, as some others do, attribute the fall of prices to improvements in methods of production.

He also admits that coincidently with and caused by the rise in gold there has been a great decline in the rates of interest, and, strangely, claims that the debtor is compensated for the rise in the value of money by the ability to convert the debt into one bearing a lower rate of interest, or, as he calls it, resorting to "debt-conversion schemes."

JONES

He does not inform us how any compensation can be made to the the debtor for the time the debt has been running, as to which it can not be converted, nor for the enhanced amount exacted from the current earnings of labor by the rise in the value of money to pay taxes and the expenses of Government, nor for the loss entailed on the debtor whose property is mortgaged on long time, where the holder of the mortgage refuses to convert it into an obligation bearing a lower rate of interest than originally contracted for. He suggests no method by which to make whole those who have lost their property through sheriff's sale by reason of falling prices and the rise in the value of money. Neither does he state how long it will be before the next confiscation is to take place, by reason of the continued operation of the cause that produced the first. But he has been frank enough to concede (what is never disputed except when the money question is under discussion) that there has been a rise in the exchangeable value of gold, and conceded its natural sequence, a fall in the rates of interest.

IMPROVED METHODS OF PRODUCTION.

In order to justify their position it becomes necessary for the advocates of continued demonetization of silver to insist that the fall of prices is not due to the rise in the value of gold but to improved methods of production.

Whatever the cause to which it is to be ascribed, the undoubted fact is that a fall of prices throughout the western world set in concurrently with the reduction of the world's money volume by the demonetization of silver. It was well understood at the time by those who had given consideration to the subject that demonetization alone would effect that result. This is manifest from an article in the London Daily News, a paper of exceedingly large circulation, quoted in the Journal of the Statistical Society of England for 1873, page 395. Referring to the adoption of the single gold standard by Germany the Daily News said :

As the annual new supply of gold throughout the world is reckoned at little more than £20,000,000 ($100,000,000), and the usual demand for miscellaneous purposes is very large, it follows that, if the German Government perseveres in its policy, the strain upon existing stocks and currencies of gold will be most severe. For a time, at least, unless the annual production of gold should suddenly increase, the money markets of the world are likely to be perturbed by this bullion scarcity, and the fall in the value of gold——

which means the rise in prices that for some time had prevailed ; of which so much has been heard, will be checked or reversed.

The yield of gold did not " suddenly increase," and the intelligent prophecy of the Daily News was fully realized, not merely to the extent of a check to the rising prices; (or, as it is styled by the Daily News, a check to the "fall in the value of gold,") but to the extent of an immediate rise in the value of that metal, and a persistent and deplorable fall in the general range of prices.

This prophecy that the "fall in the value of gold" would be checked by the demonetization of silver ; or, better, reversed by it, was welcome reading to the creditor and income classes of England and of the world.

That it was "reversed," and the value of gold appreciated, is as plain as that, one being subtracted from two, there is but one for a remainder.

The immediate fall in prices of commodities was the natural, the anticipated, and the deliberately intended result of that movement. But we are now assured that this fall is not due to any monetary

JONES

cause, but to the greater efficiency of machinery in the production of commodities.

No advocate of an increased volume of money denies that in a few departments of manufacture there have since 1873 been improvements tending to economize labor and cheapen products; but they emphatically deny and challenge proof that improvements of mere detail in the manufacture of some articles will account for the extraordinary fall of price since that time in almost every product of industry. We are also told that the development of the system of transportation, both by land and sea, have tended to lower the price of commodities to the consumers. I grant it. But we had those improvements before 1873.

The inventions made between 1873 and 1890, the period of falling prices, were no more important or radical in their effect on industry,—tended no more to cheapen commodities, than did those from 1850 to 1873, the period of rising prices. Indeed the inventions which preceded 1873 were as a whole much greater in scope, more far-reaching in result, and more revolutionary in their effects on industry, than those of the later period. All the great basic improvements had been invented, and had been incorporated with the industrial system of all civilized countries long before 1873, if we except the electric light and the telephone. We have had the steam engine, the cotton gin, and the spinning-jenny since the last century; the railroad and the steam-ship since the '30's; the telegraph, the mechanical reaper, steam-plow, and other agricultural labor-saving devices since the '40's; the sewing machine since 1854, and the Bessemer process and steel rail since 1857.

The forced construction into which their position drives the advocates of the gold standard is well illustrated in a recent number of a magazine of high standing in this country, in which I find the following:

But if it be demurred, does not a debt incurred, say, ten years ago require to-day more wheat or iron for its satisfaction than the sum could have bought when first borrowed! Certainly, but the wheat or iron represents no more labor now then it did ten years ago, and its increase in quantity stands for the new efficiency which applied science has bestowed on toil.

Observe how deftly the writer places iron, in the manufacture of which there have admittedly been some improvements, in the same category with wheat, in the production of which the improvements within any recent period have been of the most trifling character. It will be exceedingly difficult to convince the farmers of this country, whose mortgages are eating up the proceeds of their labor, that the enormous decrease in the debt-paying power of their products is made up to them in "the new efficiency which applied science has bestowed on toil."

As well might it be maintained that the rise of prices and the concurrent wave of universal prosperity, experienced after 1849, was not due to the increase of the world's money stock from the mines of California and Australia, but to some sudden, unaccountable, and complete loss of all improvements theretofore attained in the arts and industries of the world.

EFFECT OF CHECKS AND CLEARING-HOUSES.

But it is said that checks, notes, drafts, bills of exchange, and the facilities afforded by clearing-houses effect such economy in the use of money that it goes farther now than formerly, and that therefore so large a volume of money as was formerly needed is not needed at present. It is sought thus to escape the conclusion that the fall of prices is the result of a shrinkage of the volume of money, or at least to imply that if the money volume has been shrinking the agencies mentioned have served to mitigate, if not entirely to counteract, the effects of such shrinkage. This is in substance to claim that however contracted the money volume of a country may become, the system of checks and clearing-houses—on the principle of the compensating balance—will expand in a proportion directly corresponding to the contraction of the currency; that the greater the reduction of the volume of money in the country the greater the increase in the transactions of the clearing-house.

Nothing more absurd could be conceived. If this view were correct, it would make no difference whether the amount of money in circulation were large or small ; a million dollars would be as efficacious as $100,000,000, and even one dollar as effective as a million dollars; and if we suppose the last dollar to have disappeared from circulation, then, according to the sweeping and pretentious claims set up for the clearing-house system, we could dispense altogether with the use of money and rely exclusively on checks, drafts, and bills of exchange.

That checks and clearing-houses are a great convenience to commerce is not denied. They serve to a certain extent to make more effective the money volume of a country. By the clearing house system of off-setting the demands of the several banks, one against the other, and requiring payment in cash of the balances only, large amounts of loans may remain undisturbed and greater stability of industrial conditions be secured.

Clearing-houses, however, were not established primarily for the convenience of commerce, but for the profit of bankers. Whatever amounts of money are economized by means of those institutions bring compensation, by way of interest, to the banks. We may, therefore, rely upon their being utilized to the utmost under all circumstances.

But, however much checks and clearing-houses may economize the use of money, they are no novel devices. They are not some untried and newly-invented instrumentalities. Checks have been in use ever since the invention of banks. The clearing-house system was established in this country in 1853. Contributing, as it does contribute, to the pecuniary profit of the banks by making possible an economy in the use of invested money, which the banks have loaned out, and on which they are drawing interest, the system has grown with the growth of the business of the country. It will undoubtedly continue to grow, but with no greater acceleration than population and business will warrant.

As it has been a part of the banking machinery of the country for nearly forty years, and during that period has been utilized to the utmost, the conditions of its existence and utilization have long since become static conditions. The demands for currency have borne relation to the needs of business, with clearing-house facilities in full sight and operation; and at all seasons, in the adjustment of prices, those facilities have had full force and effect. Assuming that at any given period the business of the country were conducted with a given volume of money, *plus* a certain volume of clearing-house exchanges, then, at a later period, an increase of business would demand an increase in the volume of money, *plus* a proportionate increase in the volume of clearing-house exchanges; having had this system in full and effective use for forty years, it is as absurd to ascribe the *fall* of prices in the last half of that period to any economy in

JONES

the use of money effected by the clearing-house system as it would be to ascribe to the same cause the directly opposite effect—the rise of prices—that took place in the first half of the same period.

THE PROOF AFFORDED BY THE FALL OF INTEREST.

If further proof were needed that gold has risen in value, it is, as I maintain, to be found in the coincident fact of a decrease of rates of interest on first-class securities. That decrease has kept even step and pace with the rise in the value of money.

The rise in the value of gold, as shown by comparison with large numbers of articles of commerce, has been between 35 and 40 per cent. The rate of interest on gilt-edged securities shows a corresponding decline. But unfortunately for the struggling people of the country, the fall in the rate of interest on farm mortgages and on property remote from money centers has been nothing like so great, nor has it been so great as the fall in the price of agricultural lands, and in the products of labor.

I hold, therefore, that a new axiom should be added to the science of political economy; namely, that as the purchasing power of money increases, its income-producing power decreases, and in about the same ratio; and conversely, when the purchasing power of money decreases, its income-producing power increases. In other words, when prices rise interest rises; when prices fall interest falls. When money is increasing in volume and decreasing in value, prices rise, and its investment in productive enterprises becomes more profitable, and as a consequence interest rises. When it is decreasing in volume and consequently increasing in value, prices fall, investment in property and productive enterprises become precarious and unprofitable, and, as a consequence, it avoids them, and seeks investment in bonds and gilt-edged securities, aptly termed "money-futures," which for years have been increasing and continue to increase.

Some thirteen years ago I indulged in a little prophecy concerning the rates of interest. I take no great credit to myself for it, but in 1877—four years after the demonetization of silver—before the rates of interest had materially fallen, and when the same contention was made that is made now, namely, that money was cheap because interest was low, and that the policies of the country were wise because our credit stood on such a high plane, I submitted to Congress the report of the Monetary Commission, from which I quote:

Money can be borrowed readily only upon such securities as bonds which are based on the unlimited tax-levying power of the Government, or upon the bonds and stocks of first-class trunk-lines of railroad corporations, whose freight and fare rates are practically a tax upon the entire population and resources of the regions which they traverse and supply. The competition among capitalists to loan money on these more ample securities has become very keen, and such securities command money at unprecedentedly low rates. These low and lowering rates of interest, instead of denoting financial strength and industrial prosperity, are a gauge of increasing prostration. Large accumulations of money in financial centers, instead of being caused by the overflow of a healthful circulation, or even a proof of a sufficient circulation, are unmistakable evidence of a congested condition caused by a decreasing and insufficient circulation. The readiness with which Government bonds bearing a very low rate of interest are taken, instead of showing that the credit of the Government has improved, is melancholy evidence of the prostrated condition to which industry and trade have been reduced.

There need be no haste in refunding the public debt at the rates now proposed and considered low. Unless the progress of the commercial world in the policy of contracting money by demonetizing silver is checked, bonds bearing a much lower rate of interest than any yet offered will be gladly accepted by capitalists here and in Europe. When the money stock is diminishing and prices are falling, the lender not only receives interest, but finds a profit in the greatly increased value of the principal when it is returned to him. A loan of money made in 1809, if repaid in 1848, would have been repaid with an addition of 145 per cent. in the purchasing power of principal and interest, besides all the interest paid. Those who have loaned money to this Government since 1861 have already received nearly as much in the increased value of their principal as in interest, and all the probabilities are, in respect to the four per cent. thirty-year national bonds now being negotiated, if they are redeemed in gold. that more profit will be made by the augmentation in the value of principal than through interest. Indeed the signs of the times are, that the bonds of a country possessing the unbounded resources and stable institutions of the United States, payable in gold at the end of thirty years without any interest whatever. would. through the increase of the value of that metal, prove a most profitable investment.

All the facts of the situation to-day fully bear out the statements I then made.

So determined are the advocates of the single gold standard in defending the wisdom of its maintenance that facts whose existence would at ordinary times be readily admitted, are, during a discussion of the money question, pointedly denied. For example, within the past few weeks we have seen in various eastern newspaper contributions from prominent writers taking direct issue with the advocates of silver as to the prevalence of general distress throughout the country. They declare that there is no such distress, assert that they have looked for it in vain, and derisively inquire where it is.

Perhaps the best authority I can cite in response to this inquiry is the principal commercial daily journal of the east, the New York Journal of Commerce, itself one of the most ardent and uncompromising advocates of the gold standard. In an editorial article in its issue of January 11, 1890, that journal said :

FAILURES IN BUSINESS.

The public have been startled by the announcement that during the year 1889 there were 11,719 business failures in the United States, against 10,587 in 1888 and 9,740 in 1887. The estimated liabilities of last year's insolvents were $140,359,000 and the assets were $70,599,000, against $120,242,000 liabilities and $61,999,000 assets for the failures of the previous year. Thus the failures in 1889 were more in number and far greater in liabilities than for 1888, and the proportion of assets to the obligations shows that the total insolvency was more disastrous. Why in a season of profound peace, with no blighting frosts or withering droughts, and the most abundant yield from the field, forest, and mine so many in business have gone to the wall, no one seems able to answer. Many have tried their hand at a solution of the problem, and not one, as far as we can discover, has satisfied even himself with the result of his investigations.

HAS SILVER FALLEN?

In order to ascertain whether silver really has or has not fallen in value, it is necessary that all the facts be taken into account and the situation looked at from a correct point of view. If a person be seated in a boat that is headed to the stream and wishes to test whether or not he is making headway he must keep in view not the stream, but the shore. The occupant of a railroad car who observes a moving train on a contiguous and parallel track, frequently thinks his own train at a stand-still, when in fact it may be in motion. Whenever a rise or fall appears to take place in the price of any one article or commodity, that is to say whenever a difference takes place in the relation which that article bears to money—all other commodities remaining unchanged—such difference must naturally and properly be attributed to changed conditions affecting the commodity, and not to a change in the value of money. But wherever there is a fall in prices throughout the whole range of commodities then it is clear that this change is mainly due to a change in the value of money. Such however is the force of education and habit that the masses of the people are slow to suspect any change in the standard by which they have been accustomed to gauge or measure all values. Indeed they find it difficult to understand how un-

JONES—4

50

der any circumstances any change can take place in it. Having their eyes fixed on the standard, and on that alone, they naturally attribute to the articles measured, and not to the standard, any differeuee that may seem to arise in the relation they bear to each other.

But the apparent is not always the real. Nothing seems more warranted by the evidence of our senses than that the earth is a stationary object, while the sun revolves around it. For thousands of years the world was convinced of the truth of the geocentric theory of the universe, and millions of men have lived and died in the confident belief that this planet was immovably fixed in space, while the sun was a rolling and over-shifting body. Even yet, among the mass of mankind, so ever-present is this impression, derived from ocular demonstration, that in spite of the declarations of science, the world continues in common use the phrases which originally described the process that took place, as men understood it; hence we speak of the "rising" and of the "setting" of the sun. In the same way we speak of the rise or fall in the value of commodities, without being particular to note whether the change that has taken place is strictly a change in the value of the article itself or a change in the money with which its value is measured. Perhaps I can best illustrate my meaning by an allegory:

THE BATTLE OF THE STANDARDS. THE ALLEGORY OF THE CLOCKS.

In an ancient village there once stood a gold clock, which, ever since the invention of clocks had been the measure of time for the people of that village. They were proud of its beauty, its workmanship, its musical stroke, and the unfailing regularity with which it heralded the passing hours. This clock had been endeared to all the inhabitants of the village by the hallowed associations with which it was identified. Generation after generation it had called the children from far and wide to attend the village school. its fresh morning peal had set the honest villagers to labor; its noonday notes had called them to refreshment; its welcome evening chime had summoned them to rest. From time immemorial, on all festive occasions, it had rung out its merry tones to assemble the young people on the green; and on the Sabbath it had advertised to all the countryside the hour of worship in the village church. So perfect was its mechanism that it never needed repair. So proud were the people of this wonderful clock that it became the standard for all the country round about, and the time which it kept came to be known as the gold standard of time, which was universally admitted to be correct and unchanging.

In the course of time there wandered that way a queer character, a clockmaker, who being fully instructed in the inner workings of time-tellers, and not having inherited the traditions of that village, did not regard this clock with the veneration accorded to it by the natives. To their astonishment he denied that there was really any such thing as a gold standard of time; and in order to prove that the material, gold, did not monopolize all the qualities characteristic of clocks, he placed alongside the gold clock, another clock, of silver, and set both clocks at 12 noon. For a long time the clocks ran along in almost perfect accord, their only disagreement being that of an occasional second or two, and even that disagreement only at rare intervals, such as might naturally occur with the best of clocks. But the Council of the village, in their admiration for the gold clock, passed an ordinance requiring that all the weights (the motive power) of the silver clock, except one, be removed from

JOHN

it, and attached to those of the gold clock. Instantly the clocks began to fall apart, and one day, as the sun was passing the meridian, the hands of the gold clock were observed to indicate the hour of 1, while those of the silver clock indicated 12.15. At this everybody in the village ridiculed the silver clock, derided the silver standard, and hurled epithets at the individual who had had the temerity to doubt the infallibility of the gold standard.

Finally, the divergence between the clocks went so far that it was noon by the gold standard when it was only 6 a. m. by the silver standard, so that those who were guided by the gold standard, notwithstanding that it was yet the gray of the morning, insisted on eating their mid-day meal, because the gold standard indicated that it must be noon. And when the sun was high in the heavens, and its light was shining warm and refulgent on the dusty streets of the village, those who observed the gold standard had already eaten supper and were preparing for bed.

But this state of things could not last. It was clear that the difference between the standards must be reconciled, or all industry would be disarranged and the village ruined.

Discussion was rife among the villagers as to the cause of the difference. Some said the silver clock had lost time; others that both clocks had lost time, but the silver clock more than the gold; while others again asserted that both clocks had gained time, but that the gold clock had gained more than the silver clock.

While this discussion was at its height a philosopher came along and observing the excitement on the subject remarked, "By measuring two things, one against the other, you can never arrive at any determination as to which has changed. Instead of disputing as to whether one clock has lost or another gained would it not be well to consult the sun and the stars and ascertain exactly what has happened."

Some demurred to this because, as they asserted, the gold standard was unchanging and was always right no matter how much it might seem to be wrong; others agreed that the philosopher's advice should be taken. Upon consulting the sun and the stars it was discovered that what had happened was that both clocks had gained in time but that the gain of the silver clock had been very slight, while that of the gold clock had been so great as to disturb all industry and destroy all correct sense of time.

Notwithstanding this demonstration, there were many who adhered to the belief that the gold standard was correct and unchanging, and insisted that what appeared to be its aberrations were not in reality due to any fault of the gold clock, but to some convulsion of nature by which the solar system had been disarranged and the planets made to move irregularly in their orbits.

Some of the people also remembered having heard at the village inn, from travellers returning from the East, that silver clocks were the standard of time in India and other barbarous countries, while in countries of a more advanced civilization gold clacks were the standard. They therefore feared that the use of the silver clock might have the effect of degrading the civilization of the village by placing it alongside India and other barbarous countries. And although the great mass of the people really believed, from the demonstration made, that the silver standard of time was the better one, yet this objection was so momentous that they were puzzled what course to pursue, and at last advices were consulting the manufacturers of gold clocks as to what was best to be done.

Now our gold standard men are in the position of those who first refuse to look at anything beyond the two things, gold and silver, to see what has happened, and who, when it is finally demonstrated that all other things retain their former relations to silver, still persist that the law which makes gold an unchanging standard of measure is more immutable than that which holds the stars in their courses. If they will compare gold and silver with commodities in general, to see how the metals have maintained their relations, not to one another but to all other things, they will find that instead of a fall having taken place in the value of silver, the change that has really taken place is a rise in the value of both gold and silver, the rise in silver being relatively slight while that of gold has been ruinously great. And those who do not shut their eyes to the truth must see that the change of relation between the metals has been effected by depriving silver of its legal-tender function, as the want of accord between the clocks was brought about by depriving the silver clock of a portion of its motive power—the weights. The only thing that has prevented a greater divergency between the metals is the limited coinage by the United States—the single weight that, withheld from the gold clock, prevented its more ruinous gain.

THE PURCHASING POWER OF SILVER IN 1873 AND 1889.

If I can show that for a period of seventeen years, since its demonetization in 1873, silver has lost none of its purchasing power, none of its command over commodities; that is to say, if I can show that 412½ grains of silver to-day, uncoined, and shorn by hostile legislation of its principal element of value—the money use—will buy as much as would 412½ grains of silver in 1873 (when our silver dollar bore a premium over gold) of all the articles that enter into the daily consumption of the people, it must be manifest that silver has not fallen in value.

I present a table which I shall ask to have inserted in the RECORD as part of my remarks, showing the purchasing power of 412½ grains of silver, nine-tenths fine, in 1873 and 1890, respectively, so far as concerns several leading articles of daily consumption. The table is as follows:

Comparative purchasing power of 412½ grains silver, nine-tenths fine, in 1873 and 1890, respectively.

412½ grains silver would buy—	1873.	1890.
Wheat .... bushels..	0. 87	0. 88
Corn .... do ...	1. 84	1. 97
Cotton .... pounds..	5. 32	6. 71
Beef, mess .... barrels..	0. 05	0. 05
Pork, mess .... do ...	0. 07	0. 06
Lard .... pounds..	12. 89	11. 75
Butter .... do....	5. 40	4. 83
Cheese .... do ...	8. 69	6. 94
Sugar .... do ...	9. 80	10. 34
Eggs .... dozen..	4. 27	5. 36

From this table it conclusively appears that while in 1873 the standard silver dollar of 412½ grains, which then bore a premium over the gold dollar, would purchase four-fifths of a bushel of wheat; to-day the same quantity of silver, without the advantage of coinage

JOHN

and merely as bullion, will also buy four-fifths of a bushel of wheat—
the only difference between the figures for the two years being that
at the present time 412½ grains of silver bullion, as will be seen by the
table, will buy a fraction of a bushel more than would 412½ grains of
coined silver in 1873.

If, then, silver has fallen, it is manifestly not in its relation to wheat.

By the same table it is shown that the silver dollar of 1873, containing 412½ grains of silver, nine-tenths fine, would purchase one
and eight-tenths bushels of corn ; in 1890, a like number of grains of
silver, uncoined and estimated at its gold value, will purchase one
and nine-tenths bushels of corn. Here again the advantage is
slightly in favor of the 412½ grains of silver bullion of 1890. This
shows conclusively that silver has not fallen in its relation to corn.

The figures of the same table show that in 1873 a coined silver dollar of 412½ grains would buy 5½ pounds of cotton ; to-day 412½ grains
of uncoined silver will buy 6¾ pounds of cotton. From this it appears that silver has not fallen relatively to cotton, the great staple
of universal use, but that, on the contrary, it has advanced somewhat in its purchasing power when compared with that article.

In order to present the question from another point of view I submit another table showing the number of grains of silver that are
required in 1890 and the number which were required in 1873 to buy
a bushel of wheat, a bushel of corn, &c., by which it will even more
clearly appear that silver has not fallen in value in respect to commodities.

*Comparative purchasing power of silver bullion, in grains nine-tenths
fine, in 1873 and 1890, respectively.*

Articles.	1873. Legal tender.	1890. Commodity.
	Grains silver.	*Grains silver.*
Wheat..............................per bushel..	474. 3	468
Corn ....do....	223. 9	209. 25
Cotton..............................per pound..	77. 55	61. 42
Beef, mess..........................per barrel..	8, 662. 5	7, 560
Pork, mess ....do....	5, 465. 62	6, 750
Lard ....per pound..	31. 97	35. 1
Butter...................................do....	76. 31	89. 1
Cheese ....do....	47. 44	59. 4
Sugar, refined............................do....	42. 07	39. 82
Eggs................................per dozen..	96. 52	76. 68

From this table it will be seen that in 1873 it required 474 grains
of standard silver, in the form of coined dollars, to buy one bushel
of wheat ; in 1890, only 468 grains of standard silver (and that merely
in bullion form, or in other words, at its market value) are required
to buy a bushel of wheat. This does not show that silver has fallen
in value, in its relation to wheat, but, on the contrary, that it has
risen in value.

In 1873 it required 224 grains of silver to buy a bushel of corn ;
to-day only 209 grains of silver are required to buy the same quantity. These figures fail to prove that silver has fallen in value, in
its relation to corn. On the contrary, again, it has risen.

In 1873 a pound of cotton could not be had for less than 77½ grains
of silver ; to-day the same pound of cotton can be bought for 61

grains of silver. Silver, therefore, has not fallen, but risen in value in its relation to cotton.

In 1873 96 grains of silver were required to buy one dozen eggs; to-day only 76 grains of silver are required to buy the same quantity of eggs. Silver therefore has not fallen but risen in value, in its relation to eggs.

These comparisons might be continued with the same results as to a great majority of the articles entering into general use.

These figures demonstrate that in its relation to all commodities that enter into the daily consumption, silver has not fallen in value, but, as is clearly seen, while holding a remarkably steady ratio to commodities, has slightly increased in value, as is shown by the fact that a less number of grains of the metal are to-day required to purchase the same quantity of the commodities mentioned than were required in 1873.

In relation to what, then, is it that silver has fallen? As it has not fallen in relation to commodities, there remains but one thing in relation to which it can be said to have fallen, and that one thing is gold. The phrase "the fall of silver" is the ingenious and cunning invention by which it is sought to cast on that metal the discredit of depreciation rather than subject gold to the suspicion of any change whatever. The term to correctly describe what has taken place would be "the rise of gold;" but that term is scrupulously avoided, as implying that gold does not remain immovably fixed. That gold has risen, however, admits of no doubt, except to those who willfully shut their eyes to facts of common observation. The true test of the increasing or decreasing value of any one thing is not to compare it with any other one thing, but with a large range of commodities generally dealt in. It is not of so much importance to know how much gold can be bought with a given amount of silver, as it is to know how much bread, how much meat, and how much clothing can be bought, and how much of all the things that are necessary to the comfort and well-being of the people can be bought with that amount of silver.

PROOF THAT GOLD HAS RISEN.

In order to demonstrate that gold has risen, I will bring side by side the gold prices of a number of leading commodities of commerce in 1873 and 1889, respectively, and the amount in silver bullion that in 1889 would purchase an equal quantity of the same commodities, by a table prepared at my request by the Bureau of Statistics of the Treasury Department.

JOSES

Average export prices of the following named domestic commodities for the years ending June 30, 1873 and 1889.

| Commodities. | Unit of quantity. | Average price of the year ending June 30 — | | | |
| | | 1873. | | 1889. | |
		In currency.	In gold.	In gold.	In silver bullion.
Bacon and hams	Pounds	$0.088	$0.077	$0.084	$0.108
Butter	...do	.211	.184	.166	.212
Cheese	.. do	.130	.113	.092	.118
Corn	Bushels	.017	.539	.508	.650
Cotton :					
Unmanufactured, not sea Island.	Pounds	.188	.164	.099	.127
Cloth, colored	Yards	.106	.145	.065	.083
Cloth, uncolored	...do	.162	.142	.068	.067
Iron and steel:					
Bar-iron	Cwt	5.480	4.781	3.183	4.074
Pig-iron	...do	2.498	2.181	.953	1.220
Railroad-bars	...do	4.114	3.592	2.169	2.776
Lard	Pounds	.092	.080	.076	.097
Leather	...do	.253	.221	.185	.237
Rice	...do	.071	.062	.055	.070
Sugar:					
Brown	Pounds	.092	.080	.056	.072
Refined	...do	.116	.101	.066	.084
Wheat	Bushels	1.312	1.145	.874	1.119
Wheat-flour	Barrels	7.565	6.604	4.703	6.020

What does an examination of this table show ? It shows beyond dispute that gold has risen in value.

A bushel of wheat that, according to the figures of the Bureau of Statistics cost $1.14 in gold or silver in 1873, and which, as will be seen by the table, still commands $1.12 in silver bullion, will to-day bring only 87 cents in gold.

A pound of cotton that in 1873 cost the purchaser, in gold or silver, 16 cents, and which still commands 13 cents in silver bullion, will bring only 10 cents in gold.

A pound of cheese that in 1873 cost the purchaser 11¼ cents in gold or silver, and which now brings 12 cents in silver bullion, will bring only 9 cents in gold.

A barrel of flour which in 1873 cost the purchaser $6.60 in gold or silver, and which to-day commands $6.02 in silver bullion, will bring but $4.70 in gold.

A pound of butter that in 1873 brought 18.4 cents in gold or silver, and now commands 20.8 cents in silver bullion, will bring but 16.6 cents in gold.

Notwithstanding that 412½ grains of uncoined silver will to-day buy as much of the leading articles of commerce as the coined gold dollar would buy in 1873, yet the advocates of the gold standard characterize it as a 72-cent dollar. Then the gold dollar of 1873 was a 72-cent dollar. If the gold dollar of to-day be an honest and equitable dollar, that of 1873, which was worth much less, was a swindling and dishonest one; and if gold continues to advance as it has been advancing, and with the declining output of that metal there is no reason why it should not, it will be but a short time before any other kind of dollar whose value may be equal to that of the present gold dollar will be stigmatized as a swindling 72-cent dollar. There never was a dollar coined that did not legally and practically contain 100 cents. But the creditors stigmatize a dollar of the value of the gold and silver dollar of 1873 as a 72-cent dollar. May not the debtors, with much more propriety, denounce the gold dollar of to-day as a 140-cent dollar?

According to the admissions of the royal commission of England, the gold dollar of to-day is to the producers of this country, measured by their products, already at a premium of between 30 and 40 per cent. over the gold dollar of 1873. The advocates of the gold standard have no sympathy with our farmers and manufacturers who have to pay, in commodities, a premium of 30 to 40 per cent. on gold, to meet their engagements, but express extreme anxiety at the bare possibility that a few importers might have to pay even a small premium in any form. They insist that the money system of a population of 65,000,000, shall, like an inverted pyramid, be made to rest upon its apex in order to enable a few importers, most of whom are residents of foreign countries, to make their payments abroad in gold.

Verily, Mr. President, the single gold standard is an expensive luxury for our people to maintain.

Those who deride silver as a money-metal indulge in feeble attempts at sarcasm by inquiring why we do not advocate the use of tin and brass as money. They speak and write as though the idea of using silver as money were a recent discovery or invention of people engaged in silver mining. They also ignore the fact that the standard silver dollar of the United States, which, with much satisfaction, they stigmatize as a 72-cent dollar, requires a gold dollar to obtain it. It is worth a gold dollar in London, in Berlin, in Vienna, in Saint Petersburg, in Madrid, in Havana, and in all countries having commercial relations with the United States. It can at once be exchanged into the money of any country with only the slight deduction of cost of shipment to this country—as is the case in the United States with notes of the Bank of England, which are redeemable in gold.

Our silver dollar is not money in foreign countries—and it is to our advantage that it is not—for were it money anywhere else than in this country, we could not rely on its remaining here to maintain that steadiness of prices indespensable to prosperity. But if any of our silver dollars are found abroad, let no one suppose he can get them by tendering 412½ grains of silver bullion for each dollar. He will find it will cost him precisely as much gold as it passes for in the United States.

SOME EFFECTS OF THE RISE OF GOLD.

If a cotton planter in 1873 owed $10,000 he could then have paid it with 60,975 pounds of cotton. To-day, by reason of the increased command which gold has over commodities, it would take 101,010 pounds of cotton to pay that $10,000; notwithstanding that the money in which the debtor has paid the interest has each year become more valuable than it was at the time he contracted to pay it.

The cotton manufacturer of the East who in 1873 owed $10,000 could then have paid it with 70,422 yards of uncolored cotton cloth; to-day owing to the rise in the value of gold it would require 147,059 yards to pay that debt, without taking into account the amount lost by the debtor in the greater sacrifice he had year by year to make to pay the interest.

The farmer of the North and West who in 1873 owed $10,000 could

JONES

then have paid it with 8,733 bushels of wheat; to-day it would require 11,446 bushels of wheat to liquidate that debt, though he, too, has year by year been "cinched" through the progressive increase in the value of the money in which the interest has been paid. Or he could, in 1873, have paid his debt with 1,514 barrels of flour; to-day it would take 2,126 barrels of flour to pay the same debt.

The property of the country is fast passing into the hands of the creditors, and if the iniquitous system is not reversed the condition of our American farmers will be that of the farmers of gold-standard countries. Instead of owning their farms they will be tenants and rent-payers—a condition but little in advance of that which prevailed in feudal days.

Machiavelli, describing a turbulent period in the history of Florence, said:

The people perished, but the brigands throve.

The brigandage of the Middle Ages, whether in Italy or elsewhere, was a criminal defiance of law, but it was pursued at some risk, and under manifest disadvantages. The brigand took his life in his hands. He knew that his calling was unlawful ; and, although ruthless in his work, the method by which he exacted ransom of his occasional victim was less destructive to the prosperity of the community than the legalized brigandage of to-day by which, through a vicious system of money, the great mass of the people are despoiled of their property. The distinguishing characteristic of the brigandage of the nineteenth century is that it scrupulously observes all legal forms, and is conducted in the name of honor, honesty, good morals and "sound finance." Mortgages are foreclosed only in accordance with law, and the unearned increment which results from the increased and increasing value of the money is transferred from the debtor to the creditor, with punctilious regard for the statutes.

The demands of the brigand were enforced with guns and pistols; those of the creditor are enforced with bonds and mortgages; both exactions cruel and unjust, one by violence, the other by law. But, in the latter case, so indirect is the method of operation that many of those who are benefited by it are unaware of the perpetration of any wrong. So subtle is the process that the change seems to be only a change in the price of commodities, and thousands of men who would scorn consciously to exact from any one more than a just return for money loaned are beneficiaries of this vicious and ruinous system.

With regard to the great body of the working masses it is sometimes said they have no cause for complaint, that their condition now is better than ever before.

But, Mr. President, it is not enough that men are better off than they have been. When we reflect that nine-tenths of the inventions and improvements constituting all the material features of the civilization of this century have been made by working men, it is manifest that they are entitled to much more of the comforts and convenience of life than are now accessible to them. By watchful, repeated, and aggressive efforts through their trade organizations, the workingmen in many branches have been enabled to keep wages from sinking, and occasionally to secure an advance; but, during a period of falling prices, what is gained in this way by those who are kept at work is lost to the working class as a whole by the remission to idleness of part of their number.

The statisticians who seem to be employed by some propaganda to

JONES

prove by figures that prosperity prevails, point exultantly to the fact that the wages of the working people seem constantly to have increased while prices are falling, and they cite this to prove that low prices are consistent with prosperity. They leave entirely out of the account the large numbers of workmen who of necessity are relegated to idleness on account of the lack of profit in business.

If you go into the workshops of any large manufacturing enterprise, while prices are low and lowering, and ask the managers what they now do when a strike occurs among the workmen, they will tell you they find it impossible to shut down, because they have contracts extending through time that they must fill, but, they add, "We pay the wages demanded and we reduce the number of the employed."

If there are a thousand workmen employed, getting $2 each per day, that would be a wage fund of $2,000 a day. If, when prices fall and business becomes dull, the employers should want to reduce the pay of each workman to $1.50 a day, and if the workmen, by striking, should prevent that decrease, and if, then, 25 per cent. of their number should be discharged, the loss to the working class, as a body, and to the community at large, would be the same as though the wages were reduced to $1.50 a day. Until these people who present statistics can show us how many laborers are left out of employment there is no possibility of arriving at any correct conclusion as to what the wage fund is and how much wages are paid.

The loss to society is much greater when 25 per cent. of the people are unemployed than if all continued at work upon a 25 per cent. reduction of wages, because the relegation to idleness of 25 per cent. of the workmen reduces the producing force, and lessens correspondingly the aggregate annual production.

THE INTEREST OF THE MINING STATES IN THE REMONETIZATION OF SILVER.

Those who in the Senate and in the other House of Congress, represent mining constituencies are taunted with the selfish purpose of advancing the interests of their own States at the expense of those of the country. It is sought to discredit the State which I have the honor in part to represent on this floor, on the ground that the people, being largely silver miners, have a personal interest in the remonetization of silver.

The silver miners, Mr. President, need no defense here or elsewhere. They have asked no favors from the Government, and ask none now. They are bold, adventurous, and self-reliant men, who have wandered across alkaline deserts, and over pathless mountains, braved the assaults of hostile savages, the miasma of the Isthmus and the storms of the Cape, and have planted the flag of a high civilization on the western confines of this Republic. No more patriotic or public-spirited class of citizens can be found within the borders of the Union. Their business is an honorable one. When they entered upon it they, in common with other citizens, had the warrant of time, and the authority of all writers and thinkers on political economy, for the belief that silver was, and would ever be, a money metal, entitled to that full credit which from time immemorial had been accorded to it. Silver, equally with gold, had been consecrated by all the ages to the money use, and was dedicated to such use by the Constitution of the United States.

When the Constitution declared that Congress should have power " to coin money and regulate the value thereof" and that "no State shall * * * make anything but gold and silver coin a tender in payment of debts," it warranted the belief on the part of all who adopted the calling and undertook the business of mining, that gold and silver

JONES

would continue to be money metals in the sense in which they had been for thousands of years in the past. The silver miners were warranted in presuming that when the Constitution esteemed so highly the legal-tender function in the two metals, gold and silver, as that it prohibited the States from making anything a legal tender except coin of those two metals, it would not warrant the Congress of the United States in taking from one of those metals the power of legal tender and conferring that imperial function exclusively on the other. Silver mining is a business requiring for its successful prosecution skill, experience, and energy, while nine-tenths of the gold of the world has come from placers; requiring neither organization, capital, nor skilled labor.

The production of gold is much more a matter of accident and much more liable to fluctuation than is the case with silver. The silver miners therefore had a right to believe that so long as 23.22 grains of pure gold should be entitled to recognition as one dollar, 371.25 grains of pure silver would continue to be entitled to like recognition as one dollar, and would possess the legal-tender function as such, for the liquidation of all debts, public and private. On the strength of this warranty of the Constitution, and of the unbroken experience of the ages, large sums of money were invested in mining property and in the employment of labor to develop the mines of the country. On the strength of this belief and conviction, shared in by all the people of the United States, that gold and silver would both remain the money metals of the world, debts to an enormous extent were incurred, and it was confidently believed that both metals would for all time be available for the payment of those debts.

The silver-miners had learned from the history of mining, as well as from hard and bitter experience, that the mines might at any moment cease to yield, in which case their occupation would be gone and the capital invested would be a total loss. But they did not suppose that the verdict of all time would be reversed, or that the implied warranty of the Constitution of the United States would be disregarded. They did not believe that either one of the money metals would ever be demonetized. And if a doubt had entered their minds on that subject, they would naturally suppose that gold rather than silver would be demonetized, gold being too limited in quantity to answer alone the purposes of money in a rapidly advancing civilization; its yield being uncertain and capricious and the prospect of a continued and sufficient supply becoming less from year to year.

But, Mr. President, the degree of special interest which the mining States have in this measure is not to be compared with that of the other States of the Union.

According to the report of the Director of the Mint, the total quantity of silver produced in the United States in the eleven years from 1878 to 1888 inclusive was 406,210,000 fine ounces. According to the same authority the commercial value of that silver was $436,260,000, and the coinage value $525,145,000. A very simple process of arithmetic shows that the difference between the commercial and the coinage value of that silver was $88,885,000, or an average of $8,080,544 each year. Assuming that amount to have been the annual difference between the coinage and commercial value of silver for the five years preceding 1878, we must add to the $88,885,000 the sum of $40,402,220, making a total of $129,287,220 as the amount which the silver miners, not of Nevada but of the whole United States in the seventeen years ending 1889, lost by the demonetization of silver.

Having thus demonstrated in dollars and cents the degree of selfishness which, as is charged, is the motive of the miners in advocating the remonetization of silver, let us glance at the degree of selfishness which may be said to impel other classes of the community to advocate the same cause.

THE INTEREST OF THE NON-MINING STATES IN REMONETIZATION.

The price of cotton for the year 1873, in gold or silver (then of equal power), was 16.4 cents per pound. The price in 1889 was 9.9 cents.

The yield of cotton for 1889 was 7,000,000 bales, or 3,500,000,000 pounds.

Had not silver been demonetized that cotton would have brought as good a price to-day as it did in 1873. At the price of 1873 the account would have stood 3,500,000,000 pounds, at 16.4 cents, $574,-000,000. At the price of 1889 the account stands 3,500,000,000 pounds, at 9.9 cents, $345,500,000, showing a loss in debt-paying and tax-paying power on cotton alone (only one article of merchandise) in the single year 1889, by reason of the fall in prices caused by the demonetization of silver, of $227,500,000.

Having shown that the loss to the silver miners by the discount on silver for the seventeen years from 1873 to 1889 was less than $130,000,000, it will be seen that the loss in one single year to the cotton planters of the United States is greater by $90,000,000 than the total loss for the entire seventeen years to the silver miners of the country.

But inasmuch as the cotton crop of 1889 was exceptionally large, I will, for the purpose of my computation, discard it, and assume instead that an average yield for the years between 1873 and 1889 would be 5,000,000 bales per annum—which is a fair average and by no means high—5,000,000 bales, of 500 pounds each, are equal to 2,500,000,000 pounds.

At the price of 1873 the result of each year would be 2,500,000,000 pounds, at 16.4 cents, $410,000,000.

According to the figures given by the Bureau of Statistics the average price received each year of the seventeen was 13.1 cents per pound; 2,500,000,000 pounds, at 13.1 cents per pound, equal $327,000,-000, showing a difference of $83,000,000; that being the average each separate year for seventeen years, or a total sum for the entire period of $1,411,000,000, which represents the loss in debt- and tax- paying power suffered by the cotton planters by reason of the demonetization of silver.

This is the enormous tribute which has been exacted of the cotton industry of this country in behalf of the gold "standard," and of those who, for their own pecuniary advantage, cunningly induced the Congress of the United States to demonetize silver. This is the sum which the planters of this country have lost in debt-paying and tax-paying power by that mad act of folly. As will be seen at a glance, it is a loss vastly in excess of that suffered by the silver States in the discount on the price of silver bullion.

So that, if the silver miners are taunted with having a personal interest in the success of the movement for the full remonetization of silver, the cotton planter must be placed in the same category, and with ten-fold more reason.

A like computation with regard to wheat will show a loss in debt-paying and tax-paying power of not less than $100,000,000 a year to the farmers of the North and West, by reason of the demonetization of silver—a total of $1,700,000,000 in the article of wheat alone in seventeen years.

JONES

Thus a loss, wholly unnecessary, of more than $3,000,000,000 in debt-paying and tax-paying power is shown to have been inflicted on the farmers and cotton planters of this country.

In comparison with this enormous loss to farmers and planters, how paltry is the loss of $8,000,000 a year suffered by the silver miners.

But, however large the direct loss to the debtors and to the country by reason of falling prices, the losses that are indirect are of infinitely greater magnitude, and stand out like a great mountain of wrong superimposed upon the most deserving class in the community, whose interests it should be the paramount duty of Government to protect, a wrong more calamitous in its consequences than any of the multitudinous wrongs which a shrinking volume of money inflicts upon society.

THE ENORMOUS LOSS OF POTENTIAL WEALTH THROUGH INVOLUNTARY IDLENESS.

The political economist, Mr. President, deals with property *in esse*, and producers employed. I propose for a moment to deal with property *in posse* and producers unemployed. The wealth which the political economist discusses is realized wealth; that to which I now briefly invite your serious consideration is the wealth that might be, and would be, brought into existence were the energies of all the people utilized. For, while it has attracted but little attention from writers on economic science, it will be found upon examination that the non-employment of its members is incomparably the greatest loss which an increase in the value of money and the consequent disorganization of industry inflicts on society.

The great writers and thinkers on economic subjects discuss with care the elements that enter into the production and distribution of wealth. They follow in detail the manufactured article through all its stages, from the crude material to the finished product; and, when completed, they conduct it through the intricate channels by which it reaches the hands of the consumer. The greatest consideration is bestowed upon the labor employed and the wealth resulting therefrom, but scarcely any thought is given to the immeasurable mass of potential wealth not produced, but lying latent in the brains and hands of the millions who are condemned to involuntary idleness.

While no mere sum in arithmetic can represent the enormous loss suffered by a nation through this cause, let us see whether we can arrive by figures at an approximate conception, at least, of the loss of wages which it entails upon the working masses, and the corresponding loss of wealth to the country.

The most thorough and painstaking investigation into the conditions of labor in this country has been that which for many years has been conducted by the Massachusetts Bureau of Labor. Its work has been universally admitted to be free from bias, and devoid of all attempt to establish any special hobby, or to force, by figures, the proof of any preconceived theory.

SOME STATISTICS OF THE UNEMPLOYED.

An examination of the work of that bureau shows that, in 1837, there were 816,470 persons engaged in wage earning in the State of Massachusetts. Of those, 241,589, or nearly 30 per cent., were idle during some part of the year—ranging from one to six or more months. The average of their unemployed time was about four months, or one-third of the year.

Now, 240,000 people idle for one-third of their whole time is equivalent, in money loss, to the total idleness of one-third of that num-

JONES

ber, or 80,000 people, for the entire year. The whole number of persons enrolled for labor in the State being 816,470, this is equivalent to the total idleness of one-tenth of the people engaged in all occupations.

If a number equivalent to one-tenth of the people in all occupations are idle twelve months in the year in a State like Massachusetts, where labor is better organized, better classified, and more efficiently ordered than elsewhere in this country, it can not be presumed that any other State of the Union will exhibit a smaller proportion of unemployed laborers.

The Census Report of 1880 states the number of persons employed in all occupations as 17,392,099, out of a population of 50,155,783, or a percentage of 34.68 of the entire population. Our present population being not less than 65,000,000, if we assume, as we are warranted in doing, that a like proportion of the population is engaged in occupations of all sorts, it is clear that we have to-day a working population of 22,254,000 persons.

Accepting as correct the careful deductions from the Reports of the Massachusetts Bureau of Labor that a number equivalent to ten per cent. of the people are always out of employment we find that at the present time there are 2,250,000 persons involuntarily idle in this country. How faintly does the term "the army of the unemployed" describe this vast number of eager and willing men seeking in vain the opportunity to earn a livelihood for themselves and families.

Were the business of the country in the active condition in which it could not avoid being if our money system were perfectly adjusted to industry, and if employers were competing for laborers with the same degree of eagerness that laborers are competing for employment, the average wage of a day for a working man would not be less than $2. This would make but the moderate sum of $50 a month for each workman, which, under the most thrifty system of household economy, can not be considered more than enough for the support of an American family.

THE WAGE LOSS FROM INVOLUNTARY IDLENESS.

By multiplying the number of persons thus shown to be idle, by this moderate average wage, we arrive at the amount of $4,500,000 as the daily sum which is lost to the wage earners of the United States by the non-employment of labor. This is a money loss of $27,000,000 a week, $117,000,000 a month, or the amazing sum of $1,404,000,000 a year. A saving of this sum for a year and three months would pay our entire national debt. This being the loss in a single year, we can imagine (making due allowance for difference in the numbers of the population) how stupendous has been the loss to the nation during the past seventeen years, a loss exceeding incomparably all other losses whatsoever.

If a crop of wheat be lost, it is appropriately noted as a public misfortune; if a city be burned down, or swept away by flood, it is properly regarded as a great national calamity, and the sympathies of all the people go out in unstinted measure to the sufferers. But here is a loss as real and as deplorable as any ever caused by flood or fire—a loss whose consequences, while not so apparent, are as destructive to national prosperity as the burning of ten cities, or the occurrence of one hundred and forty Johnstown disasters every year, and always to the people who can least afford it. Yet it passes almost wholly unheeded except by the sufferers.

A war that would take a million of men from industry and deprive the country of the production which would result from their labors, would be regarded as a calamity of unsurpassable magnitude, yet a shrinkage in the volume of money relatively to population withdraws much more than that number from productive pursuits, and without the salutary discipline and restraints of military life, subjects them to conditions of which the unavoidable results are poverty and crime.

Imagine, Mr. President, the unhappiness, discontent, and even despair implied in the mere statement that 2,000,000 men are constantly out of employment; (or, what amounts to the same thing, that three times that number are idle for four months in the year!) Imagine, what it means to the working people of this country to be deprived of the enormous sum of $1,400,000,000 a year.

But, aside from the effect on the individual, what benumbing consequences are entailed upon the nation by the idleness of so large a number of its people. The loss of the wealth which the labor of those men might have created is a loss never to be retrieved. When the money volume of a country is sufficient to keep prices from falling, and thus to encourage capital to seek productive enterprises, in which labor is employed, every willing man is kept at work, and no country can enjoy any higher degree of prosperity than when all its people are employed, and the products of their labor equitably distributed.

Much, I believe, of the prejudice against silver money arises from an idea, conscientiously entertained, by many, that gold money has the greater "intrinsic value." I shall, therefore, Mr. President, at the risk of being a little abstruse, discuss that point.

THE MEANING OF VALUE.

No discussion of the subject of money can be intelligently conducted without a correct conception of the meanings attaching to the terms employed. For a misconception of those meanings is the root of much of the confusion and difficulty by which the subject is surrounded.

"Value" is a word which, of necessity, is more frequently used—and, I will add, more frequently misused and misunderstood—than any other employed in the discussion of economic science. Volumes have been written upon it, and yet, from the daily misapplication of the word in leading magazines and newspapers, it is evident that its meaning is very imperfectly understood.

The idea involved in the word "Value" is so broad and pervasive that within the limits of a speech it would be impossible to discuss it in all its bearings. I shall not, therefore, at this time, do more than present what I conceive to be a basic definition of it.

Value is human estimation placed upon desirable objects whose quantity is limited, and whose acquisition involves sacrifice. In order that an object may have value it must not only be the subject of human desire, but there must be a limitation of its quantity, and its acquisition must demand a sacrifice from him who would obtain it. The term "intrinsic value" is used by many writers with a total disregard of the idea involved in the word value. An article may have estimable qualities that are intrinsic, but no article whatever can have intrinsic value. Its "value" is the mental estimation of its qualities, as modified by the limitations of its quantity and the amount of sacrifice necessary to obtain it. In other words, value is subjective, not objective. In economic discussion, however, value is treated as though it resided in the object, rather than in the mind, and while, for convenience, I may occasionally use it in that sense, it is important to bear in mind the distinction.

JONES.

In that acceptation, value is usually divided into value-in-use, and value-in-exchange. Certain esteemed qualities of an object may make it of great value-in-use; but unless its acquisition demand sacrifice, it can have no value-in-exchange. It is only with this class of value that economists deal. No matter how important the intrinsic qualities of any article may be, if there be no limitation of its quantity and its acquisition requires no sacrifice, it can have no value in the sense in which the word "value" is used in political economy. The air has qualities inestimable to mankind; it must be regarded as incomparably the most useful of all the objects of human desire; yet it has no value because there is no limitation of its quantity. By reason of its universality and accessibility, air requires no sacrifice to get it. If, however, circumstances should render air limited in quantity it is conceivable that it might become of surpassing value. A man confined in the "Black Hole" of Calcutta would give a fortune for free access to air. So water, where freely obtainable, without sacrifice, although indispensable to life, has no value in the economic sense—no value in exchange. But when not so obtainable, as in populous cities, where sacrifice of time and labor would be necessary to obtain it from river, lake, or spring, people pay for the convenience of having it in their homes. The indispensable prerequisites of value in all objects are utility—either actual or attributed—combined with limitation of quantity and the sacrifice necessary to be made in order to obtain it.

But value is not a property inhering in any article itself. It is not intrinsic. If the value were inherent or intrinsic it could not be taken away.

To illustrate: A generation ago the cradle with which wheat was harvested was said to possess intrinsic value. It was undoubtedly one of the most useful of all the articles needed by man. All that was then in that machine is in it still, yet the value is gone. Had the value been something that was intrinsic, had it resided in the object, and not in the mind, that cradle would still be worth all that it ever was. So, on the other hand, an article may possess most estimable qualities, but if those qualities are not known or recognized by the human mind the article will have no value.

A few years ago cotton seed had no value as an article of general commerce. To-day it is exceedingly valuable, because it has been found to possess estimable qualities not before suspected.

Indeed so strongly does the idea of value rest upon the estimation of the mind that it is not even necessary for an article to possess in reality any desirable quality whatever in order to have value. It will be sufficient if such quality is popularly attributed to it. Numbers of instances could be cited in which there was present no element of value except limitation of quantity, added to a mere belief, or conception of the mind, that the article had desirable qualities. Many will remember that a few years ago a herb called "Cundurango" was introduced into this country from Central America. It was generally believed to possess healing qualities in cases of cancer, and so came to have great value. As soon as this popular illusion was dispelled the article ceased to have even the slightest value.

Land being indestructible and irremovable, is believed to be the embodiment of the idea of intrinsic value. Take, then, a lot on Madison avenue, New York; it is worth perhaps a thousand times as much as a lot of equal size in a village remote from the city. What proportion of its high price is derived from what is called its greater "intrinsic" value? A lot on that fashionable thoroughfare has no intrinsic attribute, or quality, that is not equally the attribute or quality of the village lot. The difference in its value, or, more correctly, the difference in the estimation in which it is held, as compared with that attaching to the village lot, is derived wholly from circumstances that are extrinsic, not from qualities that are intriusic.

The action of society in utilizing land in the neighborhood of the city lot by building up around it gives that lot a value greater than one of equal size elsewhere.

But in order that a thing may subserve a useful or beneficent purpose it is not necessary that the quality which enables it to subserve that purpose should be intrinsic or inhereut in the thing itself.

To apply this reasoning to the subject under discussion—whatever intrinsic qualities the metal, gold, may possess, they confer no force whatever on gold-money.

The money of a country is that thing, whatever it may be, which is commonly accepted in exchange for labor or property and in payment of debts, whether so accepted by force of law, or by universal conseut. Its value does not arise from the intriusic qualities which the material of which it is made may possess, but depénds entirely on the extrinsic qualities which law, or geueral consent, may confer.

Money is of transcendent importance to civilization. It is the physical agency to which society has assigned the function of measuring all equities, and it is the sole agency upon which that incomparable fuuction has been conferred. It is in terms of money that society computes the material value of all human sacrifice, alike the highest effort of genius and the daily toil and sweat of the millions who labor.

In order to measure equitably the natural and inevitable mutations in the value of other things, money should itself be of unchanging value. That is to say, any given amount of mouey should, so far as human foresight can regulate it, require at all times an equal amount of sacrifice for its acquisition. Thus, in the case of a contract made to-day, requiring the payment of a dollar twelve months hence, that dollar when due should exact from the debtor precisely that amount of sacrifice, and no more, which would be required had he paid the debt the day after contracting it.

No one will deny that the most important quality that money can possess is that it shall truthfully measure and state equities.

As I have shown by the figures heretofore cited, gold has risen in value between 30 and 40 per cent. since the demonetization of silver. It is not therefore so faithful a measure of value as is silver, which as illustrated by a variety of examples, has maintained almost uudisturbed its relation to commoditics.

THE VALUE OF MONEY, AS SUCH, NOT IN THE MATERIAL BUT IN THE STAMP. MONEY IS AN ORDER FOR PROPERTY AND SERVICES.

The logic of the situation, and the reasoning of all the leading authorities on money, lead irresistibly to the conclusion that its value does not reside in the matcrial, but in the stamp; in other words, on the legal-tender function impressed on that material. It is an order for property and services.

JONES——5

Aristotle, writing of money, says:

Money by itself * * * has value only by law, and not by nature; so that a change of convention between those who use it is sufficient to deprive it of all its value and power to satisfy all our wants.

And again he says:

But with regard to a future exchange (if we want nothing at present) money is, as it were, our security that it may take place when we do want something.

John Locke, in "Considerations," etc., regarding money, published in 1691, says:

Mankind, having covenanted to put an imaginary value upon gold and silver, by reason of their durableness scarcity, and not being very liable to be counterfeited, have made them, by general consent, the common pledges, whereby men are assured, in exchange for them, to receive equally valuable things to those they parted with, for any quantity of those metals; by which means it comes to pass that the intrinsic value regard in those metals, made the common barter, is nothing but the quantity which men give or receive of them; they having, as money, no other value but as pledges to procure what one wants or desires.

Baudeau, reputed one of the most eminent of an early school of French economists, says:

Coined money in circulation is nothing, as I have said elsewhere, but effective titles on the general mass of useful and agreeable enjoyment which cause the well-being and propagation of the human race.
It is a kind of a bill of exchange, or order payable at the will of the bearer.

Adam Smith says:

A guinea may be considered as a bill for a certain quantity of necessaries and conveniences upon all the tradesmen in the neighborhood.

Jevons's "Money and Exchanges," chapter 8, says:

Those who use coins in ordinary business need never inquire how much metal they contain. Probably not one person in two thousand in this kingdom knows, or need know, that a sovereign should contain 123.27447 grains of standard gold. Money is made to go. People want coin, not to keep in their own pockets, but to pass it off into their neighbors' pockets.

Henry Thornton, in his work on Paper Credit, says:

Money of every kind is an order for goods. It is so considered by the laborer, when he receives it, and it is almost instantly turned into money's worth. It is merely the instrument by which the purchasable stock of the country is distributed with convenience and advantage among the several members of the community.

John Stuart Mill says:

The pounds or shillings which a person receives are a sort of ticket or order which he can present for payment at any shop he pleases, and which entitle him to receive a certain value of any commodity that he makes choice.

McLeod, Elements of Banking, Chapter I, says:

When persons take a piece of money in exchange for services, or products, they can neither eat it, nor drink it, nor clothe themselves with it. The only reason why they take it is, because they believe they can exchange it away whenever they please for other things which they require.

On that view of money McLeod feels justified in styling it credit, and he quotes in support of such a use of the term credit, Burke's description of gold and silver as "the two great recognized species that represent the lasting conventional credit of mankind."

Prof. Francis A. Walker, Money, Trade, etc., page 25, speaking of carved pebbles, glass beads, shells and red feathers, used as money in certain countries at certain times, says:

They were good money, though serving no purpose but ornament and decoration. They were desired by the community in general; men would give for

JONES

them the fruits of their labor, knowing that with them they could obtain most conveniently in time, in form, and in amount, the fruits of the labor of others. '

On page 30 he says:

Men take money with the expectation of parting with it; this is the use to which they mean to put it.

Again, Mr. Walker says:

Money is that which passes freely from hand to hand throughout the community, in final discharge of debts and full payment for commodities, being accepted equally without reference to the character or credit of the person who offers it, and without the intention of the person who receives it to consume it, or enjoy it, or apply it to any other use than, in turn, to tender it to others in discharge of debts or payment for commodities.

Even Bonamy Price, who is wedded to the gold standard, in his Principles of Currency, says:

Gold, in the form of money or coin, is not sought for its own sake, as an article of consumption. It must never be regarded as valuable except for the work it performs, so long as it remains in the state of coin. It can be converted at pleasure into an end, into an article of consumption, by being sold; till then it is a mere tool.

How many people ever so "convert" it that earn it?

The great philosopher, Bishop Berkeley, one of the most acute reasoners, in my judgment, that modern times have produced, in the "Querist," published in 1710, propounds the following pertinent and suggestive questions:

Whether the terms "crown," "livre," "pound sterling," etc., are not to be considered as exponents, or denominations? And whether gold, silver, and paper are not tickets or counters for reckoning, recording, or transferring such denominations? Whether, the denominations being retained, although the bullion were gone, things might not nevertheless be rated, bought, and sold, industry promoted and a circulation of commerce obtained?

Dugald Stewart, professor of moral philosophy in the University of Edinburgh, in his Lectures on Political Economy (Part I, Book II), said:

When gold is converted into coin, its possessor never thinks of anything but its exchangeable value, or supposes a coffer of guineas to be more valuable because they are capable of being transferred into a service of plate for his own use. Why then should we suppose that, if the intrinsic value of gold and silver were completely annihilated, they might not still perform, as well as now, all the functions of money, supposing them to retain all those recommendations (durability, divisibility, etc.) formerly stated, which give them so decided a superiority over everything else which could be employed for the same purpose. Supposing the supply of the precious metals at present afforded by the mines to fail entirely the world over, there can be little doubt that all the plate now in existence would be gradually converted into money, and gold and silver would soon cease to be employed in the ornamental arts. In this case a few years would obliterate entirely all trace of the intrinsic value of these metals, while their value would be understood to arise from those characteristical qualities (divisibility, durability, etc.) which recommend them as media of exchange. I see no reason why gold and silver should not have maintained their value as money, if they had been applicable to no other purposes than to serve as money. I am therefore disposed to think, with Bishop Berkeley, whether the true idea of money, as such, be not altogether that of a ticket or counter.

Appleton's Cyclopedia, defining money, says:

Anything which freely circulates from hand to hand, as a common acceptable medium of exchange in any country, is in such country money, even though it ceases to be such, or to possess any value in passing into another country. In a word, an article is determined to be money by reason of the performance by it of certain functions, without regard to its form or substance.

JONES

Bastiat, in his "Harmonies Economiques," describing money, uses the following illustration:

You have a crown piece. What does it mean in your hands? If you can read with the eye of the mind the inscription it bears, you can distinctly see these words: Pay to the bearer a service equivalent to that which he has rendered to society. Value received and stated, proved and measured by that which is on me.

No words could more correctly describe the unit in a properly regulated system of money. And notwithstanding the attempt to discredit silver coinage, no piece of money, as I have already shown, would better answer, by its steadiness of value, this description of Bastiat's than would the American silver dollar if silver were re-monetized.

So far as it applied to gold Bastiat's description was much nearer accuracy in his day than it is in ours. In his life-time the mints of France and of the Continent were open for the coinage of silver equally with gold, and the money supply of the world was not constantly narrowing by being limited to the yield of a single metal whose annual output would hardly more than meet the demand for the arts.

Were Bastiat alive at this time he would reform his description so as to make it read as follows: "You have an American gold piece. You have had it hoarded in a bank vault for fifteen years. What does it mean in your hands? If you can read with the eye of the mind the inscription it bears, you can distinctly see these words: 'Pay to the bearer 50 per cent. more service than he has rendered to society; value not received or stated on me, but resulting from a cunning manipulation of the law of legal tender, through the influence of the holders of gold and of obligations payable therein, and as a reward to the bearer for having had this money hid away and for depriving society of its use for seventeen years.'"

When people are found everywhere working for money and not for the things which they really need, it is clear that they are working for money, not because of the material of which it is composed, but because it is an order for property which they can at any time obtain by parting with the money. To modify and elaborate Bastiat's description of the crown piece, it might be said of the Money Unit of the United States under a properly regulated system:

"You have a dollar. What does it mean in your hands? If you can read with the eye of the mind the inscription it bears, you can distinctly see these words: To all to whom this may come: Greeting. This is a dollar—a unit of money—part of the great instrumentality created by society to effect the multitudinous exchanges of property and services among men. The amount of its command is constant, because the increase in the volume of money is regulated by the sovereign authority of the nation, with strict regard to the increase of population and demand—hence the value of this unit remains unchanging through time. It is an order for all property on sale, and all services for hire; the proportionate amount of such property and service to which its possessor is entitled being fixed by the universal competition to get it."

GRESHAM'S LAW.

Many persons fear an outflow of gold from the operation of what is known as "Gresham's law," namely, that "bad money will expel good." Sir Thomas Gresham, a financier of Elizabeth's time, stated that if a number of the gold or silver coins of any given denomination were deprived of part of their pure metal, and so made cheaper than the remainder, a successful circulation of the coins thus deprived would result in the melting up or exportation of the coins of standard weight. Writing of this, Mr. Jevons ("Money and the Mechanism of Exchange," American edition, page 84) says:

> Gresham's remarks concerning the inability of good money to drive out bad only referred to moneys of one kind of metal. * * * The people, as a general rule, do not reject the better, but pass from hand to hand indifferently the heavy and the light coins, because their only use for the coin is as a medium of exchange. It is those who are going to melt, export, hoard, or dissolve the coins of the realm, or convert them into jewelry and gold leaf, who carefully select for their purposes the new heavy coins—

and avoid the light or abraded coins.

There is, however, a theorem which applies to all money, but which was recognized long before Gresham's time—although it has been erroneously called an "extension" of the law or theorem of Gresham.

That theorem is this: If, in any country, there are two forms of money, each of which is a full legal tender, and one of which can be obtained with less sacrifice than the other, the one requiring the least sacrifice will be the cheaper, and if the unit of that cheaper money will perform in every respect the same function in the payment of debts and settlement of all obligations that can be performed by the dearer money, then, for obvious reasons, the cheaper money will come into universal use, and the dearer money will disappear. But it does not follow that the cheaper money is bad money nor the dearer money good money.

The best money is always the money of the contract, that is to say a money whose dollar, whatever it may be made of, is equal in value to the dollar of the contract. If the money of the contract is the cheapest money, then that is the best money, that is the honest money, and that is the only tolerable money.

If that be the sort of "cheap" money that drives out the dear money, then manifestly the dear money is bad money.

A distinguished official of the Government, who was before a committee of this body the other day, insisted that the proposed Treasury notes should be redeemed in the "best money." I asked him what was the "best money." "Why," he said, "the money that is worth the most." Now, it strikes me, Mr. President, that if you have borrowed a dollar, and, through a badly regulated money-system, are made to pay a dollar worth 25 per cent. more than the dollar you borrowed, you are not paying the best money, but the worst money; not an honest dollar, but a swindling and dishonest dollar.

THE CREDITORS' DEMAND FOR THE "BEST MONEY."

The creditors tell us that all they want is "good money." They and their friends glibly insist that all obligations must be paid in "the best money." This is the delicate and plausible euphemism resorted to in order to gloss over and, if possible, hide from the world the odious and repulsive fact that what the creditors always want is the *dearest* money—the money that costs the people the most sweat and toil to obtain and which, as time passes, grows dearer and dearer.

This cry for "the best money" is at last beginning to be recognized for what it is—the cunning device of creditors to "catch the conscience" of the people and play upon the sense of fairness that characterizes the great mass of mankind. These interested parties

JONES

affect to believe that gold is, by nature, the only money metal, ignoring the fact that until silver was displaced by hostile legislation it was, and for four thousand years had been, the principal money metal of the world. But they will no longer be permitted to hide their sinister purpose under the cloak of a demand for the "best money." The masses of the people are aroused on this subject and are beginning to understand it.

According to all fair canons of construction the best money should be and is a money of unchanging value, a money that exacts from the debtor the same amount of sacrifice that he bargained for, and which is all that the creditor is equitably entitled to receive. In other words, the money of the contract, not a money whose exactions are increasing at the rate of 2 per cent. per annum. As McCulloch says, debts being stated in dollars and cents, it is not possible for the creditor openly to augment his debtor's obligation by changing the figures of the debt.

But, Mr. President, while they can not change the figures of the debt, they are enabled, by a crafty manipulation of the money-volume, to do that which, to the debtor, means the same thing; as the following story will illustrate:

A usurer of the coarser type had lent $10,000 on a neighboring farm, for which amount he took the farmer's note, secured by a mortgage on the property. He coveted the farm, and in his anxiety to secure it took his banker into his confidence. He informed the banker that he wanted to get possession of this farm, but it would bring $15,000 under the hammer, and he did not care to pay so much for it. "I have a subtle chemical," said he, "by which I can obliterate from the note and mortgage all trace of the rightful amount ($10,000), and that done, I can insert $15,000. Then, with the genuine signatures on the note and mortgage I can bring suit, and as the farm will not bring more than the face of the note, I shall succeed to the property."

His friend, the banker, however, advised against this course, which he characterized as not only dishonest, but vulgar, and as subjecting the perpetrator of the act to serious penalties. "Honesty" said the banker, "is the best policy." "But," he continued, "I can suggest a plan by which you may accomplish the same end without running counter to law, or the views of society. Why not join our propaganda in advocacy of 'honest money.' Gold is decreasing in quantity, and as the world has been ransacked for it in vain, it is likely to continue decreasing. If we can strike down the twin metal, silver, and devolve the entire money function on gold, it will double the purchasing power of money. Then the foreclosure of your mortgage will be sure to take your neighbor's farm, and probably leave him in your debt besides. Instead of being punished for this, you will receive the plaudits of the 'best society' for the *finesse* you have displayed and the firm stand you have taken in favor of honest money, and you will take high rank among the wisest and most conservative of our financiers.' If your neighbor makes any objection to your action, you may be able to secure his incarceration as a lunatic, but if not, he will come to be regarded in the community as a dishonest 'crank' who wishes to pay his debts in a depreciated money; for it is the constant and assiduous care of our guild to teach that only the dearest money, that which is the most difficult for the laborer, the farmer, and the mechanic to get, is honest money, and the dearer it is the more honest it is."

JONES

ALL MONEY SHOULD BE LEGAL TENDER.

To be of the fullest service to civilization whatever medium is used to do the work of money should have full money power; that is to say, it should be a legal tender. It is not sufficient that it will satisfy the demands of the Government for taxes.

Whatever is given out by the Government in payment for services rendered (and there is no other way by which payments can be made from the Treasury) should carry with it to him who has rendered the service and receives the payment, the absolute assurance that in any need, or in any contingency, it will serve him as money. There is no other means by which society can be saved from the effects of panics and monetary crises.

With a watchful and intelligent regulation of the money volume, and with the legal tender function attached to everything that is in use as money, and doing the money work, so that it will serve as a universal solvent, panics will be impossible. Under present conditions when panics come, credit money—money not endowed with the legal-tender function, which, under ordinary circumstances, has always been accepted, is refused, and thousands of millions of dollars' worth of property have been confiscated by creditors, because of the scarcity of legal-tender money. As time advances and the method of doing business on credit becomes more and more extended, the more palpable it becomes that society can preserve itself from these periodical convulsions only by broadening, under proper regulation, the legal-tender basis on which, in the ultimate analysis, all business rests.

MONEY A MEASURE OF VALUE.

There is nothing upon which the prosperity and happiness of a people so much depend as on the integrity of their measure of values.

It is universally admitted that after the making of a contract requiring future delivery of a specified number of pounds, bushels, or yards of any commodity, it would be subversive of all equity and justice to change the capacity of the measure constituting the foundation of the contract. These measures, to be just, must remain unchanged. But how infinitely more important is it that money, which is the measurer of all other measures, should itself be unchanged? Of what avail is it that the subordinate measures remain intact while this, the supreme measure, into which all others are finally resolved, is constantly changing? Its " value " is but another name for its purchasing or measuring power. In the case of all time contracts, therefore, any change in the value of money works a destruction of equity, and one of the first objects of society should be to maintain and enforce equities at all times and in all places. This, so far as money can effect it, can only be done by an intelligent regulation of the volume in circulation.

In a note to his edition of Adam Smith's "Wealth of Nations," (page 502) Mr. J. R. McCulloch says:

Money is not a mere commodity, it is also the standard or the measure by which to estimate and compare the value of everything else that is bought and sold, and if it be, as it undoubtedly is, the duty of Government to adopt every practicable means for rendering all foot-rules of the same length, and all bushels of the same capacity, it is still more incumbent upon it to omit nothing that may serve to render money, or the measure of value—a measure which is undoubtedly of the greatest importance—uniform or steady in its value.

Though a measure of value, money is a much more complicated instrument than a yard-stick, pound weight, or bushel. Were it not so, a child could fix value with the same precision as an adult.

JONES

As value resides in human estimation, it will frequently vary as to the same object. An intending purchaser may have one notion of the value of an article, an intending seller another. Money, therefore, is a measure of value in the sense that it is a measure of the average human judgment—from which results price. As Mr. McCulloch says, no means known to science or art should be left untried to keep the value of money unchanging.

When a man promises to deliver money or makes any time contract, he makes a mental calculation as to what amount of property, or of the product of his labor, will enable him to meet his engagement. If he be a farmer, raising wheat, there passes through his mind the sacrifice and toil necessary to raise it, and the quantity he can raise; if a cotton manufacturer the cost of spindles, of looms, and steam-engines; the wages of labor and interest on plant.

I knew a cotton manufacturer who wanted $10,000. His business was good. He was sober, honest, and industrious; had a thorough knowledge of his trade; managed his employés himself, and took the greatest pains to conduct his business on the strictest business principles. He wanted the money to make some improvements in his factory. He knew how many spindles and looms he had; how much could be done with a pound of cotton, how much it cost, and how much each spindle and loom would do. He said to a capitalist, "I know all about cotton spinning and weaving, and do not know anything about this thing called money, but I want $10,000 of it." Said he, "My cloth is worth 10 cents a yard; it sells at that rate in unlimited quantities by wholesale; nobody can make it any cheaper; but I am not working a gold mine; I am not manufacturing legal-tender paper money, and the only way I can get money is to swap my cotton cloth for it. I will give you my note for 100,000 yards of cotton cloth, which will be equal to $10,000, and will pay 2 inches a yard each year as interest."

This was satisfactory to the capitalist, and the note was made, signed, and delivered accordingly, and the improvements were made in the factory.

During the year everything went smoothly; the spindles and looms worked well, repairs to machinery were light; cotton had been bought at proper rates; and no improved processes had been discovered or applied in the production of cotton-cloth. There was no hitch in any direction.

At the appointed time, the creditor called for his cloth. "I am ready," said the debtor, "to pay the hundred thousand yards of cotton cloth, with interest." When he came to measure it off, however, he was astounded to find he was short. Some painful suspicions crossed his mind. It seemed as though somebody had either robbed him of cloth, or else he had not manufactured as much of it as he had supposed. There did not seem to be so many yards of the cloth as there ought to be. He knew he had used the same number of pounds of cotton that it had been his custom to use for 100,000 yards of cloth and for 200,000 inches of cloth in addition; still, there was no denying the fact of the shortage.

He measured it again and again, and had finally to admit that he was unable to keep his engagement. This was a source of great distress to him. He could not sleep that night. But, the creditor being importunate, the cotton manufacturer next morning borrowed enough cloth from the proprietor of a neighboring factory and paid his obligation. But, not understanding how his carefully made plans had failed, and in order to avoid similar mistakes in the future, he had an examination made of the yard-stick and found that instead of being 36 inches long the yard-stick he had used was 40 inches.

In talking the matter over with his neighbor, the cotton manufacturer said: " I have been swindled; they 'rung in' on me a lengthened yard-stick, by the measurement of which I have paid my debt, and I have therefore paid in reality more than I contracted to pay."

" Well, " said the friend, " I do not see that you are any worse off than I am. I borrowed as much as you did, and at the same time; but I agreed to pay my debt in money, and gave my note for $10,000 with interest. The increased command over cloth acquired by the dollars I have had to pay, caused by the demonetization of silver, has juggled me out of as much cloth as you have been juggled out of by the lengthened yard-stick. But you have one recourse; you can put into the penitentiary the man who ' rung in' the lengthened yard-stick on you, while the increase in the value of the dollar which I have paid has been effected in the name of the gold standard and honest money, and leaves me without recourse. "

In its ultimate analysis, money is the yard-stick, the bushel and the pound weight of commerce.

When you shrink the volume of money, and so increase the measuring power of the dollar, you lengthen the yard-stick, enlarge the specific gravity of the pound and the cubical content of the bushel, in violation of all equities.

It is utterly impossible to secure a proper regulation of the money volume with gold alone, the yield of which has declined from an average of $130,000,000 a year between 1851 and 1873 to $105,000,000 a year between 1873 and 1889.

THE VALUE OF MONEY FIXED BY THE COMPETITION TO GET IT.

Everybody admits that the value of all other things is regulated by the play against each other of the forces of supply and demand. No reason has been or can be given why the value of the unit of money is not subject to this law.

WHAT IS THE DEMAND FOR MONEY?

The demand for money is equivalent to the sum of the demands for all other things whatsoever, for it is through a demand first made on money that all the wants of man are satisfied. The demand for money is instant, constant, and unceasing and is always at a maximum. If any man wants a pair of shoes, or a suit of clothes, he does not make his demand first on the shoemaker, or clothier. No man except a beggar makes a demand directly for food, clothes, or any other article. Whether it be to obtain clothing, food, or shelter—whether the simplest necessity or the greatest luxury of life—it is on money that the demand is first made. As this rule operates throughout the entire range of commodities it is manifest that the demand for money equals at least the united demands for all other things.

While population remains stationary, the demand for money will remain the same. As the demand for one article becomes less, the demand for some other which shall take its place becomes greater. The demand for money therefore must ever be as pressing and urgent as the needs of man are varied, incessant, and importunate.

WHAT IS THE SUPPLY OF MONEY?

Such being the demand for money, what is the supply? It is the total number of units of money in circulation (actual or potential) in any country.

The force of the demand for money operating against the supply is represented by the earnest, incessant struggle to obtain it. All men, in all trades and occupations, are offering either property or services for money. Each shoemaker in each locality is in competition with every other shoemaker in the same locality, each hatter is in competition with every other hatter, each clothier with every other clothier, all offering their wares for units of money. In this universal and perpetual competition for money, that number of shoemakers that can supply the demand for shoes at the smallest average price (excellence of quality being taken into account) will fix the market value of shoes in money; and conversely, will fix the value of money in shoes. So with the hatters as to hats, so with the tailors as to clothes, and so with those engaged in all other occupations as to the products respectively of their labor.

NO ALTERNATIVE FOR MONEY.

The transcendant importance of money, and the constant pressure of the demand for it may be realized by comparing its utility with that of any other force that contributes to human welfare.

In all the broad range of articles that, in a state of civilization, are needed by man, the only absolutely indispensable thing is money. For everything else there is some substitute—some alternative; for money there is none. Among articles of food, if beef rise in price, the demand for it will diminish, as a certain proportion of the people will resort to other forms of food. If, by reason of its continued scarcity, beef continue to rise, the demand will further diminish, until finally it may altogether cease and center on something else. So in the matter of clothing. If any one fabric become scarce, and consequently dear, the demand will diminish, and, if the price continue rising, it is only a question of time for the demand to cease and be transferred to some alternative.

But this can not be the case with money. It can never be driven out of use. There is not, and there never can be, any substitute for it. It may become so scarce that one dollar at the end of a decade may buy ten times as much as at the beginning; that is to say, it may cost in labor or commodities ten times as much to get it, but at whatever cost, the people must have it. Without money the demands of civilization could not be supplied.

Money was the most potent instrumentality in the evolution of society from a low to a high plane of civilization. It is valueless to man in isolation. It is indispensable to man in organized society. It is as necessary for the proprietary distribution of wealth as railroads and steamships are to its physical distribution. The aggregate force of the demand for money in any country depends upon the numbers of the population; with a stationary population the demand is steady, with an increasing population the demand increases, and in order to maintain undisturbed the equation of supply and demand the volume of money should be increased in at least a ratio corresponding to that of the increase of population.

There are certain circumstances that to some extent disturb the relations between population and money supply, such as the broadening of the areas of population, and the multiplication of money centers. These circumstances might render necessary a larger percentage of increase in the money volume than would be indicated by the increase of the population.

But under any circumstances the smallest money-increase that will suffice to maintain the equity of time contracts is an increase corresponding to the increase of numbers of the population.

JONES

Under conditions of unvarying demand and unvarying supply the value of the unit of money would be unvarying. If as population and demand increase the supply of money be proportionately increased, there is no possibility of a change in the value of the unit of money.

The constant and unceasing effort to exchange services and all forms of property, which have but limited command over the objects of human desire, for money, that sole instrumentality that has unlimited command over such objects, is, and ever will be, eager, intense, and unwavering.

With population and consequent demand rapidly increasing how do the advocates of the gold standard expect to increase the money volume of the country in this proportion, while the yield of gold, instead of increasing in proportion to demand, is every day becoming less and less capable of meeting the requirements of the arts alone?

THE QUANTITY OF MONEY IN CIRCULATION SHOULD INCREASE IN A RATIO NOT LESS THAN THE RATIO OF INCREASE OF POPULATION.

It will be admitted that if the population of a country be increased by any given percentage there will be a proportionate increase in the demand for all articles that supply human needs. If the population increases by 3 per cent., there will be needed 3 per cent. more houseroom, 3 per cent. more furniture, 3 per cent. more food, 3 per cent. more of all things that enter into consumption. These things can only be got by a demand first made on money. Then why not 3 per cent. more money?

The present monetary circulation of this country, including gold, silver, and paper, is represented to be $1,700,000,000. As our population doubles in thirty years, the rate of increase is $3\frac{1}{2}$ per cent.

If the money volume be not increased by a proportion at least as great as this, the true relation between the supply of money and the demand for it will not be maintained. The demand increasing as the population increases, while the supply either does not increase at all or increases in a degree incommensurate with the demand, the money volume shrinks and the purchasing power of the unit becomes greater by reason of the increased keenness of competition to get it. This is but another mode of stating that the prices of all products of human labor decline. Prices falling, business ceases to be profitable, stores and work-shops close, and men are relegated to idleness.

THE QUANTITATIVE THEORY OF MONEY—THE VALUE OF EACH DOLLAR DEPENDS ON THE NUMBER OF DOLLARS OUT.

Thus by the universal competition to get it the value of the dollar is made to depend upon the number of dollars that are out. This is a principle that lies at the very foundation of the science of money. The law, stated broadly, is that the value of each unit of money in any country at any given time depends on the whole number of units in circulation in that country. The larger the number of units out, population remaining the same, the less must be the value of each unit; the smaller the number of units out, population remaining the same, the greater the value of each.

Notwithstanding the variance sometimes found between the premises and the conclusions of economic writers, there is no economist of repute who does not admit this to be a fundamental principle.

On the theory I have propounded therefore $3\frac{1}{2}$ per cent. of $1,700,000,000, or $56,000,000, is the minimum amount of money that should be added to the currency of this country during the present year.

JONES

Assuming the population of to-day to be 65,000,000 and the ratio of its annual increase 3¼ per cent., the population of next year will be 67,166,600. The percentage of monetary increase to be provided for that year should therefore be based on the increased number. And so on for each succeeding year.

I have thought best to collate a variety of citations from the most distinguished authorities on financial economy to support my contention that, *ceteris paribus*, the value of each dollar depends on the number of dollars in circulation.

John Locke, in his "Considerations," etc., published in 1690, said:

Money, while the same quantity of it is passing up and down the kingdom in trade, is really a standing measure of the falling and rising value of other things in reference to one another, and the alteration in price is truly in them only. But if you increase or lessen the quantity of money current in traffic in any place, then the alteration of value is in the money.

Locke further said:

The value of money in any one country, is the present quantity of the current money in that country, in proportion to the present trade.

The historian, Hume, says:

It is not difficult to perceive that it is the total quantity of the money in circulation, in any country, which determines what portion of that quantity shall exchange for a certain portion of the goods or commodities of that country.

It is the proportion between the circulating money and the commodities in the market which determines the price.

Fichte says:

The amount of money current in a state represents everything that is purchasable on the surface of the state. If the quantity of purchasable articles increases while the quantity of money remains the same, the value of the money increases in the same ratio; if the quantity of money increases, while the quantity of purchasable articles remains the same, the value of money decreases in the same ratio.

James Mill, in his treatise on political economy, says:

And again, in whatever degree, therefore, the quantity of money is increased or diminished, other things remaining the same, in that same proportion the value of the whole, and of every part, is reciprocally diminished or increased.

John Stuart Mill (Political Economy) says:

The value of money, other things being the same, varies inversely as its quantity; every increase of quantity lowering the value, and every diminution raising it in a ratio exactly equivalent.

And again:

Alterations in the cost of the production of the precious metals do not act upon the value of money, except just in proportion as they increase or diminish its quantity.

Ricardo (reply to Bosanquet) says:

The value of money in any country is determined by the amount existing. * * * That commodities would rise or fall in price in proportion to the increase or diminution of money, I assume as a fact that is incontrovertible. * * *

Ricardo further says:

There can exist no depreciation in money but from excess; however debased a coinage may become, it will preserve its mint value; that is to say, it will pass in circulation for the intrinsic value of the bullion which it ought to contain, provided it be not in too great abundance.

In this case Ricardo's illustration is the supposed case of a country actually using one million gold pieces each containing 100 grains. He maintains that they would be of the same purchasing power, if the Government took out 1 grain, or even 50 grains, the quantity remaining the same, but that if, from the grains so deducted, an addi-

JONES

tional number of pieces were struck, a corresponding depreciation would result.

William Huskisson ("The Depreciation of the Currency," 1819), says:

> If the quantity of gold in a country whose currency consists of gold should be increased in any given proportion, the quantity of other articles and the demand for them remaining the same, the value of any given commodity measured in the coin of that country would be increased in the same proportion.

Sir James Graham says:

> The value of money is in the inverse ratio of its quantity; the supply of commodities remaining the same.

Torrens, in his work on Political Economy, says:

> Gold is a commodity governed, as all other commodities are governed, by the law of supply and demand. If the value of all other commodities, in relation to gold, rises and falls as their quantities diminish or increase, the value of gold in relation to commodities must rise and fall as its quantity is diminished or increased

Wolowski says:

> The sum total of the precious metals is reckoned at 50 milliards, one-half gold and one-half silver. If, by a stroke of the pen, they suppress one of these metals in the monetary service, they double the demand for the other metal, to the ruin of all debtors.

Cernuschi says:

> The purchasing power of money is in direct proportion to the volume of money existing.

Prof. Francis A. Walker, in his work on "Money" (page 57), says:

> The value of money in any country is determined by the amount existing.
>
> Its [money's] power of acquisition depends not on its substance, but on its quantity. [Paulus, author of the Pandects, sixth century.]

Professor De Colange, in the American Cyclopedia of Commerce, article on "Money," says:

> The rate at which money exchanges for other things is determined by its quantity. * * *
>
> Supposing the amount of trade and mode of circulation to remain stationary, if the quantity of money be increased, its value will fall, and the price of other commodities will proportionally rise, as the latter will then exchange against a greater amount of money; if, on the other hand, the quantity of money be reduced, its value will be raised, and prices in a corresponding degree diminished, as commodities will then have to be exchanged for a less amount of money. * * *
>
> In whatever degree, therefore, the quantity of money is increased or diminished, other things remaining the same, in that same proportion the value of the whole and of every part is reciprocally diminished or increased.

A curtailment of the volume of money in a country will, *ceteris paribus*, increase the value of the money of that country. All the authorities agree that this law applies to all forms of money, whatever the material; so that it applies to paper money with precisely the same force that it applies to metallic money.

Mr. Stanley Jevons, in his work on "Money and the Mechanism of Exchange," says:

> There is plenty of evidence to prove that an inconvertible paper money, if carefully limited in quantity, can retain its full value. Such was the case with the Bank of England notes for several years after the suspension of specie payments in 1797, and such is the case with the present notes of the Bank of France.

Mr. Gallatin said:

> If in a country which wants and possesses a metallic currency of seventy millions of dollars, a paper currency to the same amount should be substituted, the seventy millions in gold and silver, being no longer wanted for that purpose, will be exported, and the returns may be converted into a productive capital, and add an equal amount to the wealth of the country.

JONES

In his Proposal for an Economic and Secure Currency Ricardo says:

A well regulated paper currency is so great an improvement in commerce, that I should greatly regret if prejudice should induce us to return to a system of less utility. The introduction of the precious metals for the purposes of money may with truth be considered as one of the most important steps toward the improvement of commerce and the arts of civilized life; but it is no less true, that with the advancement of knowledge and science, we discover that it would be another improvement to banish them again from the employment to which, during a less enlightened period, they had been so advantageously applied.

Mr. J. R. McCulloch, in commenting on the principles of money laid down by Ricardo, says:

He examined the circumstances which determine the value of money * * * and he showed that * * * its value will depend on the extent to which it may be issued compared with the demand. This is a principle of great importance; for, it shows that intrinsic worth is not necessary to a currency, and that provided the supply of paper notes, declared to be a legal tender, be sufficiently limited, their value may be maintained on a par with the value of gold, or raised to any higher level. If, therefore, it were practicable to devise a plan for preserving the value of paper on a level with that of gold, without making it convertible into coin at the pleasure of the holder, the heavy expense of a metallic currency would be saved.

It appears, therefore, that if there were perfect security that the power of issuing paper money would not be abused; that is, if there were perfect security for its being issued in such quantities, as to preserve its value relatively to the mass of circulating commodities nearly equal, the precious metals might be entirely dispensed with, not only as a circulating medium, but also as a standard to which to refer the value of paper.

In adopting a paper circulation—

Says Lord Overstone—

we must unavoidably depend for a maintenance of its due value upon the adoption of a strict and judicious rule for the regulation of its amount.

Lord Overstone further declared that:

The value of the paper currency results from its being kept at the same amount the metallic currency would have been.

Alexander Baring, in his evidence before the secret committee of the House of Lords in 1819, said:

The reduction of paper would produce all those effects which arise from the reduction in the amount of money in any country.

Prof. F. A. Walker says:

Let me repeat, money is to be known by its doing a certain work. Money is not gold, though gold may be money; sometimes gold is money, and sometimes it is not. Money is no one thing, no group of many things having any material property in common. On the contrary, anything may be money; and anything, in a given time and place, is money which then and there performs a certain function. Always and everywhere that which does the money-work is the money-thing.

Sir Archibald Alison says:

The suspension of specie payment in 1797, making bank notes a legal tender receivable for taxes by providing Great Britain with an adequate internal currency, averted the catastrophe then so general upon the Continent, and gave it at the same time an extraordinary degree of prosperity. Such was the commencement of the paper system in Great Britain, which ultimately produced such astonishing effects, and brought the struggle [of the Napoleonic wars] to a triumphant close.

THE TRUE MONEY STANDARD.

The true money standard of any country is not the material of which the money is made. The standard is not a concrete object, but a numerical relation. It is the relation between the number of

JONES

units composing the monetary circulation of the country and the numbers of the population.

It is the legal-tender function that constitutes money. It is the power which the law imparts to any material to pay debts and liquidate obligations. It can not for a moment be doubted that the money function, being conferred by the supreme authority, is the all-sufficient guarantee of the money value. There is no necessity for re-euforcing that value with any inferior value that may attach to the material on which the money stamp is placed. The money function is immeasurably the most important that can be conferred by society upon any material, and it is absurd to urge that that function is not of itself sufficient for the maintenance of the value of money. All the value that money can possibly have—the totality of value that can exist in the shape of money in any country—will attach to anything upon which the sovereign authority stamps it, whether the material on which the stamp is placed be gold, silver, paper, or anything else. Legislators or executive officers of the Government, by increasing or decreasing the volume of money, correspondingly decrease or increase the value of each unit of that money. For no matter how many or how few the units may be, the total value of the money of the country will be comprised within the total number of those units. A change in the number of the units effects a proportionate change in the value of each unit, and whatever the value of the unit may be, it is of the utmost importance that that value should remain undisturbed.

It is absurd to maintain that a gold unit, which, as time goes on, is constantly increasing in purchasing power, is a better unit than a unit of any other material that maintains unchanging value through time.

Whenever the business of the country accommodates itself to a given number of units, the only question for the Government to to deal with is to maintain that value as free from disturbance as possible; and according to all authorities on political economy that can only be done by increasing or decreasing the number of units in circulation in accordance with the demands of increasing or decreasing population.

If it be admitted that one of the most important offices of government is to see that the equities are preserved between its citizens (and if this be not so, to what purpose are our courts of equity instituted?), then it can not be denied that it is one of the highest offices of government to see that money, which measures all equities, and which must for all time continue to be the-principal measure in the service of civilized society, shall be of unchanging value. It is impossible to secure this characteristic of uniformity in the value of money if we are to select as the only material on which to stamp the money function a substance whose yearly production is becoming more and more limited, and the prospect of whose sufficient yield becomes less and less encouraging.

IF SILVER REMAIN DEMONETIZED AND GOLD CONTINUE DECREASING, WHERE IS THE WORLD'S FUTURE MONEY SUPPLY TO COME FROM?

If the distinguished authorities I have quoted are correct, that a diminution of the volume of money increases the value of the money unit—which is but another form of stating that it lowers prices and produces stagnation, distress, and discontent,—what good reason can be offered by the advocates of the gold standard for confining the business of this rapidly growing country to a basis of gold, when it is well known that the entire stocks of gold and silver together are now insufficient to serve the purpose of the world's money, and have to be supplemented and re-enforced by large issues of paper notes? Do they not reflect that the production of gold is constantly diminishing and is likely to continue to diminish? And do they not know that our population is growing at the rate of over 3 per cent. per annum and will double in thirty years? Do they mean that the money volume which serves a population of 65,000,000, and is far below the needs of that population, will suffice for the 130,000,000 of the next generation? To be sure, if we are to take no note of prices, the question is a simple one.

But prices must be taken into account. The entire money question is one of prices. When it is said that money is scarce, what is meant is that business is depressed and that money is difficult to get, at the present range of prices. Should prices fall 25 per cent. money would be found plentiful enough to conduct exchange at the lower range. But when prices fall, goods sell below cost, business is unprofitable, workshops are closed, and men are thrown into idleness. If lowering prices do not affect injuriously either the business or the prosperity of the country, then it makes no difference what the volume of money may be; a small amount will meet the requirements as well as a large amount. In that case, the gold standard is as good as any.

But if gold alone is sufficient to bear all the enormous monetary burdens of the Western world, why do the advocates of the gold standard admit the necessity for any more circulation? To be logical, instead of favoring an increase of credit money, which has always lurking within it an element of danger to the business of the community, they should demand the retirement of the $347,000,000 of greenbacks and the $350,000,000 of coined silver, and base the business of the country exclusively on what they call "honest money." If that should be done all that could happen would be a fall in prices. Judging by the experience of the past it would not be surprising if the next move of the gold-standard men would be an agitation for the retirement and cancellation of the greenbacks. Such a movement is fully in harmony with the opinions of the gold-standard advocates for the past twenty years. Indeed, the Secretary of the Treasury who took charge of the finances at the opening of the last Administration, himself a banker, recommended the demonetization of the greenbacks almost as vigorously as he opposed silver.

MONEY VALUABLE ONLY FOR THE IMPORTANT SERVICE IT PERFORMS.

Money is valuable rather for the service which it performs than for the material of which it is composed.

When we consider the transcendantly important character of the service which money performs—when we reflect that, without it, the achievement of an advanced civilization would be impossible, we can not escape the conclusion that, compared with the value of that service, the commodity value of any material on which the money function may be stamped is too trifling to merit serious attention.

This will be made clear by reflection on the necessities of the situation.

So long as society chooses to maintain the automatic or metallic money-system, it must be obvious that to escape the evils that would result from a sudden and overwhelming increase in the supply of the money-material as compared with the entire stock in existence, and the infinitely more serious evils that would result from a wholly insufficient yearly addition to that stock, it must have on hand an enormons accumulation of the metals on which the stamp is placed. It must be manifest that no material would be fit for universal acceptance for so important a function as money unless there were available so great a quantity of it that no sudden shock could be inflicted on society by ordinary fluctuations in the current yield, or in the current consumption in the arts.

But, in the nature of things, a supply sufficient to effect that result would be so enormous as practically to destroy the market value of the material as a mere commodity if the money function and use were withdrawn from it.

THE MONEY DEMAND, NOT THE COMMODITY DEMAND, THAT GIVES GOLD ITS VALUE.

Mr. Giffen the statistician of the London Board of Trade, in an article recently published in an English magazine, berating and deriding the bi-metallists, maintains that it is not the demand for gold as money, but for gold as a commodity, to be used in the arts, that determines its value.

To prove his case, Mr. Giffen states that the supply of gold is about $95,000,000 per annum, the annual demand for the arts $60,000,000, or about two-thirds of the annual supply ; while the demand for money is only $35,000,000, or about one-third that supply. He therefore argues that the art demand, being the greater of the two, contributes more largely to the maintenance of the value of gold than does the demand for that article as money. It is hardly necessary to point out the absurdity of this claim.

The commodity demand in any one year is not made upon the current year's supply, but upon the entire amount in existence, which, is estimated to be about $4,000,000,000. If the demand for the arts entirely ceased, would the addition, to the money volume, of the $60,000,000 now used in the arts produce any appreciable effect on the value of the $4,000,000,000 in existence ?

On the other hand, what is the demand on gold for the money use? All the labor and all the salable property of the western world are constantly offered in exchange for it. It is a moderate estimate to assume that each dollar is earned, demanded, and paid once a week, or fifty times in each year. This constitutes a total annual money demand of $200,000,000,000, compared with which colossal sum how inconsequential is the commodity demand of $60,000,000 in maintaining the value of gold.

 The amount of gold annually used in the arts is not very definitely ascertained, but in 1886 it was estimated by the then Director of the United States Mint to be $46,000,000 per annum. Mr. Giffen estimated it at $60,000,000. It is my opinion that the arts forage on the money-stock of gold to the extent of about the entire annual yield. The bullion or commodity value of that metal being determined by its money value, whoever desires to use it for any purpose other than money, takes the bullion at its coinage value, or else melts up the coin.

Were gold demonetized and deprived of its money function, and its demand confined solely to that arising from its adaptability for various other purposes, the present stock of that metal on hand and in use as money would, according to the estimates of the director of the mint, supply the art demand for more than seventy-five years to come. But, assuming that the estimate of the Director of the Mint is too low, and that my own is nearer the truth, there is at least fifty years' supply on hand. Were there fifty or seventy-five years' supply of any other commodity on hand in the market, what would be the commercial value of that commodity ? What would be the value of copper, of brass, or of iron, if there were fifty or seventy-five years' supply of either of those metals in the market for disposal at one time ? Nobody can pretend that any commodity of which there is an available supply on hand equivalent to the whole demand for fifty or seventy-five years can have any but the most trifling value.

Contrary, therefore, to the generally received conviction that the commodity demand is the dominating force in fixing the value of gold I maintain and insist that the commodity demand, if entering into the account at all, is insignificant. It is the supremely important *money*-demand, as correlated to the supply, that fixes the value of all money of every description whatsoever.

The demand for gold as a commodity is limited and fluctuating, but when that metal is invested by law with the higher function of money, and thus constituted a common denominator of all values, that limited and fluctuating demand is changed to an unlimited and constant one, which fixes its value for other and inferior uses. If the commodity-demand for gold were, as many believe it to be, essential to its acceptance as money, it would be a great misfortune to society. The happiness and prosperity of the world, if not wholly dependent upon, are largely influenced by, steadiness in the value of money, and this can not exist without steadiness in its volume. Whatever demand exists for gold as a commodity can only affect the volume of money injuriously—that is to say, by decreasing it. The admonition of history is that a deficiency in the money-supply is more probable, and infinitely more to be feared than an excess, and this deficiency is, in great measure, caused by the insidious and constant encroachment, upon the precious metals, of demands for them for other than the money use. When we contrast the magnitude of the world's interests and equities, which rest on steadiness in the value of money, with the comparative unimportance of the uses of the metals as commodities, it becomes apparent that the subjection of the value of money to disturbance from the demands for gilded signs, looking-glasses, bangles and breast-pins, is an evil for which society is but poorly compensated by the benefits derived from such uses.

Whatever other quality gold may possess than as the bearer of the money function is inconsistent with the healthful and proper exercise of the task assigned it as such. Whenever any portion of the metal is used for any other purpose than money it destroys the money and thus changes the value of every unit of money in circulation, for, as already stated—other things remaining unchanged—the value of each dollar depends on the number of dollars that are out. Without forewarning, and without knowledge on the part of the people, large amounts of the money volume, on which so infinite a number of equities rest, and on the basis of which all debts and time contracts have been entered into, are, as it were, surreptitiously abstracted and appropriated to other and always inferior uses, for by far the highest and noblest use of any material upon which the money function has been conferred, is the money use. No other use can possibly be so high or so noble as that of maintaining all equities undisturbed.

It seems unworthy a highly developed civilization which, as to all subjects other than money, regulates its affairs by the application of intelligence, and bases its policies upon exact data, scientifically ascertained and correctly applied, to depend for its money system upon the accidents, make-shifts, and expedients to which primitive society, by reason of the limitation of its powers and the undeveloped condition of the human mind and hand, was compelled to resort. If the quantitative theory of money be correct—if the money standard be, as I insist it is, a steady and duly proportioned numerical relation existing between the units of population and units of money—it is the duty of society and government to see that as far as practicable that principle is put into operation.

The history of the production of the precious metals from the remotest ages demonstrates that under the automatic system of money this can only be effected by the unrestricted coinage of, and conferring the full legal-tender function on, both metals.

THE PROPOSITION THAT THE GOVERNMENT SHOULD LEND MONEY ON THE SECURITY OF REAL ESTATE.

If a change in the whole number of money units in circulation relatively to population and business do not affect the value of each unit, then no objection can be found to the proposition recently presented in the Senate by the distinguished Senator from California, which created some surprise among Senators. The resolution of that Senator contemplates a loan by the Government to holders of real estate based upon the security of the property; and the issue of a large amount of Treasury notes for that purpose. Certainly, if a dollar, in order to perform properly the money function, must have in it or back of it a dollar's worth of material, there can be no safer security found than that suggested by the Senator from California, namely, the arable land of the United States.

It is the most absolutely secure of all securities ; it can neither run away nor be stolen, it can not be burnt up, lost, or destroyed.

Arable land is, in and of itself, capable of supplying all basic wants, and must be always in demand, while gold, so far as concerns any use to which it is, or can be applied, might be dispensed with altogether, with scarcely any inconvenience to society.

Certainly money based on land would seem to be better than money based on gold. Senators who are sticklers for so-called "intrinsic value" money, and "full-value" money, should be found supporting that proposition. But it must, on reflection, be obvious that, other things remaining unchanged, whenever the total number of units of money (or dollars) in the circulation of a country increases, the value of each unit will decrease. It is an axiom of political economy that no amount of increase in the number of units of money in a country increases the aggregate value of the money of that country.

The aggregate value of the money in circulation in a country, can, *ceteris paribus*, be increased only by an increase of population and business, that is to say, by an increase in the demand for it.

If, without increase of population, the money of a country be increased from, say, $1,000,000,000 to $2,000,000,000, the effect would be not to add to the aggregate value of the money of the country, but to decrease the value or purchasing power of each unit of the money, so that it would take ten dollars to buy what had before cost but five.

GOLD, A FETICH—DEMAND FOR A STANDARD OF JUSTICE.

The history of the world affords no example of a money system regulated by human prescience and intelligent calculation. It is not too much to say that the money system of the world—the most important associative instrumentality of civilization, in so far as it is not controlled for their own advantage by the creditor classes—is practically the result of accident. We are even less logical than the ancients, for they availed themselves of the entire supply of money possible to their civilization and development. They used the full yield of both silver and gold, while we, in order to line the pockets of a privileged caste of money-lenders, reduce the money volume to the lowest possible minimum by discarding one of those metals and making all debts payable in the other.

Gold has been erected into a fetich by methods familiar to the pagan priesthood, who forbade investigation of the claims of their idol to the superstitious veneration of their followers. The quality of a universal standard claimed for gold has been set up by the classes which, like that priesthood, had interests to be served by the superstition. All things else may be subjected to the test of reason and argument, but the slightest approach to a scrutiny of the claims of gold as a much-vaunted universal standard of valuation has been repelled by interested casuists and sophists who constitute the sacred guard of the temple of the idol.

The people of this country, Mr. President, begin very seriously to doubt the sacredness of a so-called standard by which they have been robbed of thousands of millions of dollars—a standard that despoils and impoverishes the toiling masses, in order to swell the plethoric pockets of the privileged few. From all parts of the Republic we learn that the people have become aroused on this subject, that they have discovered gold to be a standard, not of valuation, but of spoliation and confiscation.

The world at large shares to a great extent in the doubts entertained by the people of this country as to the orthodoxy of the continuing worship of gold. Throughout all Europe the suspicion is beginning to make itself felt, among those who have no personal interest at stake, that the constantly appreciating value of this metal bodes no good to society, however advantageous it may be to the moneyed classes, and especially the money lenders. It begins to be feared that there may be too long a persistence in this artificial standard, and that the pressure upon the people, in the fall of prices and the increase of the burden of debt and of taxes, which multiply with time, may have serious consequences upon public order. The stock of gold, never half enough to meet the wants of the people anywhere, is year by year being drawn upon more and more for use in the arts, while the yield from the mines is decreasing, and giving no promise of any material increase from any quarter.

The pressing need of the time, the standard for which the people are calling, is a standard of equity, a standard of justice, a standard that shall measure fairly and impartially the rights of both parties to a contract, that will not wrongfully and stealthily add to the burden of the obligation on either side, that will not, under the guise of fair dealing, rob one of the parties for the benefit of the other. The first indispensable step to a realization of that standard is the full restoration of silver to its rightful position as a part of the money of the world.

In any discussion of the question, it would be uncharitable not to make allowance for the force, on many consciencious minds, of what, to the free and unprejudiced inquirer, can only be regarded as an absurd and meaningless superstition, which, notwithstanding the advance of thought in other directions, still persists in disarranging the industries and vexing the civilization of an enlightened age. It is to the strength of this obdurate superstition that we must ascribe the horror with which many minds contemplate the possible loss to the country of a part of its gold.

JONES

FEAR OF THE OUTFLOW OF GOLD.

Any prospect of the outflow of gold is regarded as the opening of a veritable Pandora's box, from which must issue forth all the evils that can afflict mankind.

It is to this fear, no doubt conscientiously entertained, that we must attribute the declaration of the President of the United States that we do not dare to tread on the edge of so dangerous a peril. It is not difficult to make the statement, but it will be very difficult to prove that we stand on the edge of any peril whatever, if most or even all our gold should go.

We heard this same apprehension expressed, and with equal, if not greater, force twelve years ago, when the silver question was before this body. We were then assured by the ablest of our so-called "financiers" that the country would be denuded of its gold and that all manner of dreadful catastrophies would result. The prospect was represented to be appalling, although I do not remember that any reasons were given to show how or why gold should leave the country, nor that any statement was made as to exactly how this country would suffer if it did leave.

For my own part, Mr. President, I regard it as a matter of very little consequence whether gold goes out or not. Certainly if, in order to retain gold, we must sacrifice justice, then I say let gold go.

It is not of so much consequence that we should retain gold for the benefit of a small coterie of importers as that we should preserve the equity of time contracts between the millions of our own people who import no foreign goods. It is monstrous to think of violating all equities in time transactions—and nine out of every ten of our domestic business transactions are of that character—for the absurd and inconsequent purpose of keeping in this country some particular commodity, whether it be designated as money or otherwise.

The hoarding or the outflow of gold is a hardship when, under the law, somebody is obliged to have it, as was the case during the war, when gold alone would pay duties on imports. Combinations to hoard gold at that time frequently involved great loss to the importer. But thanks to the silver legislation of 1878 and other legislation making our Treasury notes receivable for customs dues, no damage could now result from any attempted corner in gold.

The creditors of this country never can convince the enterprising and energetic people who form the debtor class that it is to our interest that a certain material shall be kept in the country as money, if the expense of keeping it is that the debtors shall continue to be despoiled as they have been for the past fifteen years.

If we can only retain gold at the expense of steady and unwavering prices, and at the expense of a steady and unchanging value in money, then the quicker gold goes out the better. The constantly increasing value of gold by reason of its increasing scarcity means the constantly increasing burden of all debt, and involves the final absorption of all the property of the country by the creditor classes. Under the operation of the present system, by which prices are constantly falling and money is constantly increasing in value, the surplus earnings of the people are flowing in a steady stream into the vaults of money-lending institutions, and into the pockets of creditors.

In a very intelligent article published in a late number of an influential magazine—the Political Science Quarterly—there is the significant statement, apparently derived from the best sources, that

JONES

in the year 1879–'80, one-half of all the mortgages in the State of Indiana were foreclosed.

It were better for society that property should at once be confiscated than that the great masses of the people in every community should have to struggle through years of painful and exhausting effort in the face of constantly falling prices and then in a large percentage of cases to lose their property at last. But this can not be avoided so long as we attempt to keep up what is called the gold standard. It is a necessary consequence of the gold standard that we shall have the scale of prices that obtains in gold standard countries. If the presence of gold in this country is to destroy our people, who doubts that it should go? If its presence is to result in the destruction of equity and justice, who doubts that it should go?

Nearly every witness who testified before the secret committee of the House of Commons in 1857 agreed that gold could only be held by paralyzing the business of the country. It is estimated by witnesses who testified before that committee, that in the panic of 1847, in Great Britain, the property of the country, by reason of the measures rendered necessary to maintain the single gold standard, was depreciated $1,500,000,000. I commend that report to the careful and serious perusal of the advocates of the single gold standard in this country.

Among the witnesses before the committee were John Stuart Mill, Lord Overstone, and many other men distinguished in the world of letters and finance. I am informed by the Librarian of Congress that there is but one copy of the work in the United States. It would be well worth while for Congress to order a number of copies of it printed, for there is no work with which I am acquainted that contains so much practical information as to the working of the single gold standard. According to the testimony taken before that committee, the experience of Great Britain since 1819 shows that gold alone, even when re-enforced by paper money convertible exclusively into gold, instead of being a beneficent instrument of valuation, has proved a cruel instrument of injustice.

A brief consideration of the causes which affect the movement of gold will not be out of place in this connection.

RATIONALE OF THE MOVEMENT OF GOLD.

Why is it that gold leaves one country and goes to another? For one reason only—the advantage of its owner. Whenever he can make a profit by sending it out, the gold goes; and the period when that profit can be made is indicated when the prices of goods that are internationally dealt in are either rising in the country which it leaves or falling in the country to which it goes. It is only to pay for importable goods that gold ever leaves the country in which the owner resides. Being an international money, and receivable everywhere at its full face value, gold loses nothing by transfer; hence it is sent wherever it will for the time being have the greatest purchasing power.

Whenever the general range of prices in this country of commodities internationally dealt in becomes higher than the general range of the same commodities abroad, it is manifest that then gold can be used to advantage by purchasing those articles abroad and selling them here. If the gold that goes out goes from stock that has been hoarded here, the outflow has no immediate or direct effect upon prices in this country, although, by increasing or "inflating" the volume of money abroad it assists in raising prices there, and thus tends to secure for our exported products a better price in the foreign

JONES

market. But if the gold goes from the amount that is in active circulation here, and if the void created by this outflow is not filled with other forms of money, such as silver, or paper, it results in a reduction of the volume of money in actual use in this country, while at the same time increasing the volume of money abroad.

This increase in the foreign money stock causes a rise of prices abroad, while the corresponding reduction of our currency causes a proportionate fall of prices here, hence there is a constant tendency to an equilibrium of prices of all articles of international commerce.

No outflow of gold would follow a rise of prices here except in so far as that rise affected articles internationally dealt in. No rise of prices of such articles as we do not import would tend in any way to drive out gold. If, for example, raw cotton should increase in price in this country, that fact would not tend to drive out gold, because we do not import raw cotton. But should the prices of articles of manufactured cotton rise here above what those same articles could be bought for in any foreign country our merchants would send abroad for them, provided that, after paying the freight charges and customs dues, they could make a profit on them.

So, also, if crockery-ware were made in this country, and its price should rise to, say, double the present price, then, instead of buying the American, or home-made article, our crockery merchants, finding that they could buy in England, France, or Germany cheaper than they could buy in this country, would decline to buy the American crockery, and would send abroad for any article, provided that, after paying freight charges and customs dues, they could sell it here at a profit. That would tend to increase the shipments of gold to foreign countries.

That an outflow of gold does not follow from a rise of general prices, but only of prices of articles of international trade, is manifest from the fact that if land becomes cheap in other countries, gold does not leave this country to buy it. When real estate is cheap in Brazil, or Australia, or in Germany, France, or even England, the owners of gold in this country do not send it abroad to make purchases of real estate.

So wages of labor may rise in this country, or compensation for all manner of services that must be performed here, and gold would not leave as a consequence. But if cloth were cheaper—quality considered,—in England, France, or Germany, or at the remotest ends of the earth,—than in this country, our merchants would send gold for it in order to sell it here at a profit.

Altogether too much importance is attached to the possession of a large stock of gold, unless that stock form part of the active circulation of the country. So long as it remains in circulation it sustains prices and develops industry and internal commerce. But the tendency of gold being to find the most profitable field for operation, its continued presence in the country can never be relied upon.

When we take gold from other countries prices in those countries fall, owing to the reduction of the volume of money there; and owing also to the action of the foreign banks in immediately raising their rates of discount on commercial paper and suddenly calling loans. As there is less money left in such country with which to pay for commodities, we are obliged to accept lower prices for the products we ship to it.

The larger the stock of gold, therefore, accumulated by us the lower,

JONES

necessarily, must be the price which we can receive for our surplus agricultural products.

In order to maintain parity between the metals, it is not necessary for us to have all the gold we now have; $200,000,000, or even $100,000,000 of gold, would maintain that parity. The parity between the metals can never be broken until all the gold leaves, and provided we retain one or two hundred million, the rest can not be placed more advantageously than where our languishing surplus products must be sold.

When gold leaves this country it is because prices here are rising. Prices are now lower than they have been since 1847. Must they continue declining in order that we may be able to retain all our gold? It is manifestly impossible for the people of this country to prosper with a constantly lowering range of prices. It is equally impossible for the present level of prices to be maintained with a constantly increasing demand for, and as constantly diminishing a supply of, gold. It is universally admitted that an increase in the money circulation of this country at the present time is an exigent necessity. The advocates of the single gold standard, while admitting that we must increase our money volume, the effect of which must be to maintain, if it does not raise, the level of prices here, insist that we shall let none of our gold go in order that prices abroad may rise.

Mr. BLAIR. May I ask the Senator a question?

Mr. JONES, of Nevada. Certainly.

Mr. BLAIR. Does the Senator mean to be understood that the falling of prices is an absolute demonstration of the increased value of the money without limitation?

Mr. JONES, of Nevada. I have already, in the early portion of my remarks, had occasion to state that when a fall in prices was brought about by a larger subordination of the forces of nature to the uses of man, as where the comforts and conveniences of life could be produced with less sacrifice than before, it was not an injury to society, but an advantage. In other words, if, by a certain amount of sacrifice seventeen years ago, only one pair of shoes could be produced, and if by the same sacrifice two pairs could be now produced, there would be a lowering of the price of shoes to about one-half of what it was seventeen years ago, which would be a very great benefaction to mankind.

But, as I then stated, there is one certain sign that that is not, except to the slightest extent, the cause of the present universal fall of prices. When prices fall owing to improvements in manufacture, business revives, the masses of the people are at work, those who toil find themselves possessed of more of the comforts, of the conveniences, and even of the luxuries of life than before. They are better contented with their condition, and more buoyant and hopeful than before. On such occasions money becomes more and more in demand than it was before, and instead of being hoarded is put into active and productive business where it will make a profit. But when interest falls, pari passu, with the fall of prices, it shows that the fall of prices is not due, except in the smallest degree, to improved methods of production, but to the increased value of money.

Mr. BLAIR. I was not controverting the Senator's theory as to the existing facts in this country, but I understood him to be laying down an absolute principle, applicable under all circumstances and in all times, that the fall of prices is a demonstration of the increased value of money. I supposed that the fall in prices resulting from a protective tariff was beneficial, and not an indication of an increase in the value of money, and that that fall of price was not owing to the increased value of money, but was by improved machinery and all that. So it is possible that some of the fall in prices in this country may be owing to increased facility in the matter of producion and to the beneficial operations of the protective tariff.

Mr. JONES, of Nevada. Mr. President——

Mr. REAGAN. If the Senator from Nevada will permit me, I wish to ask the Senator from New Hampshire if he means to be understood as assuming that a protective tariff reduces the value of the commodities produced?

Mr. BLAIR. I was simply asking for information of the Senator from Nevada, and he can answer that question much better than I; but the Senator from Texas understands very well that I do believe a protective tariff reduces prices.

Mr. JONES, of Nevada. Mr. President, so far as a tariff has the effect of reducing prices in any country, it is not by reason of the levying of any certain percentage of duty on the imported goods. The first effect of the tariff certainly always must be to raise prices. The fundamental theory of the tariff is—whether it be correct or not I am not now discussing—that by that tariff you place the price of manufactured goods up to a range at which they can be produced in the country in which the tariff is levied, and upon the level of the range of wages and manner of living which obtain in that country. By so doing, if you have a proper volume of money, you set all your people at work, and keep them at work at a variety of occupations. In such case every forge, furnace, and factory becomes a school, every machine-shop an academy, and every cnuuing device and invention becomes a lesson, teaching the people how to deal with the subtle forces of the universe. So far as this country is concerned the theory of the tariff is that 65,000,000 people should have a varied and complete system of manufactures, which should supply practically all their own wants, instead of an abnormal proportion of them being driven into the single occupation of farming and relying on foreign manufacturers to supply such finished products as they need. To draw out and develop the aptitudes of a people a large variety of occupations is indispensable. When all men are employed at their aptitudes new inventions multiply, progress is accelerated, and the secrets of nature are more rapidly unfolded. Hence the McCormick reaper; hence the sewing-machine, that great instrument which clothes the world, because of the discovery that the eye of the needle should be at the point; hence the air-brake, the telegraph, the electric light, and thousands of other inventions that a protected people originate and develop, which would perhaps not have been originated or might have been long delayed if it had not been for the discouragement to imports caused by the tariff, and the encouragement to our people to go into manufactures by which their varied talents are drawn out and cultivated.

There is no doubt that eventually as our conditions improve, increasing numbers of our people will by degrees emerge from agricultural and enter manufacturing pursuits. A tariff, by stimulating the organization and development of industries, trains men to greater skill and perfection of workmanship in a variety of departments, and with greater skill comes greater efficiency of labor, and so greater economy of time. In that way the prices of certain products are in time reduced: but that is not a reduction of which any one complains.

JONES

The trne canse of tho present discontent will not be found in the protective tariff, but in tbo exactions of the single gold standard.

Fifteen years ago England was on the gold standard. It is ou the gold standard to-day; yet prices in England aro 35 per cent. lower than they were fifteeu years ago. There being no reason why there should be any change in the trend of prices, so long as a fierce contest for the possession of gold shall be waged between England, France, Germany, and the United States, we are justified in assuming that a proportionate decline of prices will continue. That means a further decline of 30 or 35 per cent. in prices during the next fifteen years. Where is this tendency to stop? and if it does not stop, how long will it be before the masses of the people become the bond slaves of the creditors? It is shocking to the moral sense of mankind that a few money-lenders and bondholders should thus be able, silently and insidiously, to wreck the business of every country in the world by constantly increasing the value of the money unit.

While admitting the necessity of more monetary circulation, our gold standard friends fail to show us how it is possible for an increase in the volume of money to benefit our merchants, farmers, or mechanics if the prices that prevail in gold standard countries are to prevail here; for that is what the gold standard means for us, Mr. President. It means that the prices that rule in gold standard countries are to rule here.

The extreme indefiniteness with which the term "gold standard" is used has so befogged the relation which gold money bears to industry and commerce that people lose sight of the essential feature of that relation. It is impossible to have a clear conception of the gold standard without keeping in view exactly what is implied by the term. What men must mean in this country by "the gold standard" is not the touch of the metal, for they never touch it, and rarely, if ever, see it. The maintenance of the gold standard here simply means the maintenance here of the range of prices that prevail in gold-using countries; that is to say, that low and lowering range of prices rendered necessary by the attempt to measure the value of the constantly increasing mass of the products of industry in all the western world by the constantly diminishing volume of gold. No relief can come to the toiling masses of this country until we can lift our prices above those that now prevail in gold-using countries.

Even if our prices remain as they are and do not increase, gold will eventually leave the country if it continue to increase in value as it has been increasing during the past fifteen years. We have been enabled to maintain the gold standard here for the past twelve years notwithstanding a considerable addition of money other than gold to our currency, but we have been able to do so only because other countries have been using an equal or greater amount of money other than gold. We have been using no greater proportion of silver or paper money than other countries having the gold standard are using, hence we have been able to maintain their level of prices and still keep the metals together. But whenever we shall attempt to prevent a further fall of prices in this conutry, It will be impossible for us to retain our gold so long as prices in gold-using countries continue to decline as they have been declining. Gold will leave as quickly because of contraction abroad as of inflation here, if by "inflation" is meant a coinage of money sufficient to maintain prices at a steady level.

Should gold leave the country, then, in order to supply its place,

JONES

in order to maintain the *status quo* in prices, and prevent a further fall from the present low range, we should need to have as many dollars of silver in circulation as there are now dollars of gold. Gold would go out only because our prices were rising, and as it went prices would cease to rise. That process might continue until three or four hundred million dollars of gold had gone. In all this, where would be the disadvantage to our people?

Considering the rapidly increasing population and wealth of this country, all the silver that can be procured from the mines will be necessary to maintain the level of prices and to keep pace with the increasing demands for money. If, however, it slightly exceeds—and it could not at the utmost more than slightly exceed—the amount actually demanded by increasing population and business, the overplus of each year would take a great many years to drive gold out of the country, dollar for dollar. For, when prices here, of things internationally dealt in, are at an equilibrium with prices of the same articles abroad, gold can not go any faster than silver comes in.

IF $2,500,000 SILVER PER MONTH HAS NOT DRIVEN OUT GOLD, HOW MUCH WILL DO SO?

For twelve years past we have had a silver coinage of nearly $2,500,000 a month, yet no gold has been driven out. Having tested the capacity of that quantity of silver to drive out gold, we find that instead of driving it out its coinage has resulted rather in bringing gold in. For, to whatever cause the influx of gold may be ascribed, it is unquestionable that the gold has come, and it has needed all that gold, and all the silver that we have coined, to maintain international prices here.

It is admitted by all that gold can not go out except by reason of a rise in this country of the prices of articles of international commerce beyond the prices of the same articles prevailing abroad. It is only then that it becomes more profitable to send out gold in payment for our foreign purchases than to send out commodities—the products of our own country. Commodities will always be sent out in payment for other commodities so long as it is more profitable to send them than gold, and when, by reason of low prices prevailing abroad and high prices here, it is no longer profitable to send out commodities, purchasers send out gold, but only because it is to their advantage to do so.

Now, having seen that the coinage of $2,500,000 of silver each month was insufficient to so raise prices in this country as to induce gold to go abroad, but that on the contrary it resulted in an influx and accumulation of a large amount of gold, we may safely assume that only so much of the amount of silver which Congress shall now provide for as exceeds $2,500,000 a month will have any influence in raising prices in this country above international prices, and so providing a stimulus for gold to go abroad in payment for commodities imported into this country.

If the amount of silver which shall be now provided should be, say, $5,000,000 a month, the excess over the present coinage would be $2,500,000 a month. This, then, would be the amount that would drive out gold. As one dollar of silver would drive out no more than one dollar in gold, no more than $2,500,000 could go out monthly. That would leave in circulation the same amount of money that is in circulation now. There would still be no increase in the money volume of the country, and, with no increase in the volume of money, prices here would not rise above international prices. At the rate of $2,500,000 a month, it would take twenty years to drive

JONES

out $600,000,000 of the $700,000,000 of gold now in this country. It
would take even longer than that, because the $600,000,000 driven
out would tend to raise international prices abroad, and so check
the outflow of gold from here.

Mr. McPHERSON. Will the Senator yield to me for a question,
or does he prefer to go on?

Mr. JONES, of Nevada. I am always ready to answer a question.

Mr. McPHERSON. I do not want to interfere with the Senator's
line of argument, or with his speech in any form, but it does seem
to me that there is something fallacious about the Senator's argument, or else my judgment and the experience of the world is all
wrong. I wanted to ask the Senator this question: If it be known
that the Government of the United States, if you please, by such an
increase of the silver coinage in this country as will be produced by
the free coinage of silver, to which theory, as I understand, the Senator is fully committed—if that be the theory of the Government
hereafter by the command of Congress, I want to ask the Senator if
he broadly and boldly asserts that no gold can be driven out of the
country to a greater extent than dollar for dollar for the silver that
comes in?

Mr. JONES, of Nevada. Absolutely; I say so.

Mr. McPHERSON. Then I want to ask the Senator another question, which seems to be pertinent. Does the Senator assert that if a
72-cent dollar, the value in bullion of a silver dollar during the year
1880, as has been furnished us by the Director of the Mint and the
Secretary of the Treasury, were coined without limit (I say without
limit, the limit being, of course, the amount of bullion that is brought
to the Treasury to be coined), and the people of this country who
have been in favor of a safe and honest currency, a currency either
gold or as good as gold, which the Treasury has been able to maintain, having forced no silver upon the people if they did not wish it,
and in that way the silver dollar having been maintained equal to
the gold dollar, I want to know, with the people of this country
to-day the holders of $500,000,000 of gold, how it is possible for the
Senator to believe that with a 72-cent dollar to take its place the
gold coin would circulate for a single week, or a single day, or a
single hour? If they have the gold will they not hold it?

Mr. JONES, of Nevada. The Senator has so involved his question
with his argument that I can scarcely get at what he wants me to
answer.

Mr. McPHERSON. The question I want the Senator to answer
is this: Will the people of this country, the financiers of this country, the banks, the moneyed men holding $500,000,000 of gold, with a
certainty of the free coinage of silver and going to a silver basis, for
that is what it means, put their gold in circulation, or will they
hoard it? Will it disappear?

Mr. JONES, of Nevada. I scarcely know what the Senator means
by a "silver basis." He talks about a 72-cent dollar. We have
never seen a 72-cent dollar. The papers in the East have told
us that the silver dollar was worth 72 cents. I recollect talking
on that subject once with some Senators in the cloak-room. During
the conversation one of the Senate pages brought me a telegram, on
which he said the telegraph messenger had told him there were 50
cents due. I gave the page a silver dollar and said to him: "I have
been informed by some very respectable and intellectual gentlemen
in here, some of them candidates for the Presidency even, that this dollar is worth only 75 cents. I do not want to cheat a little boy. Take

this out, and if the boy thinks it worth only 75 cents he can send me back 25 cents, and if he thinks it is worth a dollar he can send me back 50 cents. I will leave it to him." The page brought back 50 cents and said the telegraph boy told him he did not know what those old "duffers" in there might say, but it was as good a dollar as he wanted and was very hard to get. [Laughter.]

The Senator talks about the bullion value as though that had anything whatever to do with the value of the dollar. I have attempted to demonstrate that the material that was in the dollar has nothing whatever to do with it. Let me illustrate. Suppose the entire supply of silver of the world to-day were $60,000,000. Suppose the law limited the coinage of it to $58,000,000, and every dollar coined was at par with gold. Suppose there were a demand for half a million dollars of silver, to be used in the arts, and that the remainder ($1,500,000) of uncoined silver were barred from the imperial money use. That supposes a supply of $2,000,000 left after satisfying the requirements for coinage, and supposes only half a million dollars' demand for use in all the arts. In that case there would be a $2,000,000 supply bearing down a half million dollars' art demand, or a proportion between supply and demand of 4 to 1. Suppose that under those circumstances silver bullion went to 50 cents an ounce. Would the Senator then say that 50 cents an once was the value of the $58,000,000, and all the rest of the coined silver of the western world, while by coining another million and a half, which would be nothing to a country like this, all the silver would be at par with gold? Every ounce of silver coined in Europe and the United States is at par with gold, a thousand or twelve hundred million dollars of it to-day in France, $200,000,000 in Germany, $370,000,000 of it here. We are not dealing with the price of silver bullion, that portion of silver that is deprived of its immemorial use as money. We do not say what the commodity demand for silver may make that worth. Such a consideration has no bearing whatever on the value of money.

I will suppose that in some one county of the United States a law were passed that the wheat grown in that particular county should have no right to go through the grist-mill, and that that wheat, as it might very naturally do, being deprived of use, fell to one-half the price of the wheat grown elsewhere in the country. Would the price of the wheat of that one county thus under interdiction and denied the grist be a fair gauge by which to measure the value of the entire wheat crop of the country? Manifestly not. All we have to do is to take up the little "slack" of silver, and all of it will at once be at par with gold; then we shall hear no more about the "commodity value" of silver. That is the contention that the bimetallists make.

Mr. HEARST. It will be $1.29.

Mr. JONES, of Nevada. It will be $1.29 an ounce in one week—in three days—in fact the very moment you give it back its ancient right of coinage and restore to it its full money power. You coin of gold all that is brought to the mint, and you deny to a certain portion of silver that same long-established privilege, and then you measure the value of the whole supply of silver by that of the little fraction that is not coined, and which therefore has to find a market as a commodity.

Mr. McPHERSON. Then, if the Senator will permit me, he necessarily proposes that the Government of the United States shall take up all this "slack," as he calls it, in the surplus quantity of silver and shall use it in the coinage. The mints of Europe being closed against the coinage of silver, there is no other place where it will be coined. Now, if the Government of the United States should use all the surplus silver in the country, which has simply forced the price down since we remonetized silver in 1878 more than 20 per cent.——

Mr. JONES, of Nevada. Gold has risen 35 per cent.

Mr. McPHERSON. Then I think the Senator's argument is upon this idea and upon this plan, that after we are upon a silver basis, as we should be most assuredly, there would be no inequality in the money, because it would be all silver.

Mr. JONES, of Nevada. And no inequality between it and gold.

Mr. McPHERSON. Certainly not, because there would be no gold in circulation. But let me ask the Senator another question. While he can use his short-legged silver dollar for the payment of debts, when he comes to make a new obligation would not the price of the goods assume a price equal to the difference between gold and silver? In other words, while you can use a debased currency for the payment of debts, if a legislative decree requires that you shall accept it, you can not use it for any other purpose.

Mr. JONES, of Nevada. I can not understand the Senator. We have not provided any "short-legged" dollar. The Senator is assuming a good many facts and attempting to adjust me to them. I ask the Senator to wait until he has heard my argument, and I invite the Senator then to make reply to it.

Mr. McPHERSON. I am sorry that I interfered with the Senator.

Mr. JONES, of Nevada. It was no interference on the part of the Senator, except that I can not separate the Senator's questions from the argument and assumptions that he makes. As to the outflow of gold, as I have said, it would take a long time for even $400,000,000 of it go. The amount of gold driven out would tend to raise prices abroad by making money more plentiful there, and so check the outflow of gold from here. When Senators speak about $600,000,000 of gold being withdrawn from circulation here a question that is a little curious arises. What are these people who own it going to do with that gold after they have withdrawn it from circulation? Are they going to invest it in Great Britain? Are they going to invest it in France? Are they going to the Cape of Good Hope to invest it? If they are they will reverse the policy that English capitalists are pursuing now and have been pursuing for years—bringing their gold over here for investment. The Senator tells us that gold is to disappear from circulation. What will the owners do with it? Where and in what are they going to invest it?

Mr. McPHERSON. It will be held for a premium.

Mr. JONES, of Nevada. But who will buy it at a premium? Who needs it at all? For what purpose is it needed? Who is going to pay any premium for it? Nobody is "short" on it, and there is no law which forces anybody to have it.

Mr. President, nobody wants it enough to give a premium for it. It is only worth what is daily paid in the markets of the world and nobody is going to pay a premium for it. It is a bogie with which to frighten the people who demand reform in the currency of this country. Let them withdraw their gold.

I tell the Senator it is not the men who hoard the gold in vaults who maintain or promote the prosperity of this country, but the toilers in the wheat-fields and on the farms of the country, the men who work in the planing mills, the forges, the furnaces, the factories, and in all our institutions of industry. It is they that bring

JONES

us our prosperity, and not these people who are gambling for premiums on gold.

Let them gamble among themselves; let who lose and let who win, the people care nothing. The people of the United States are going to institute a money that shall install and maintain justice as between the citizens of this country, and they will not be impeded. I can tell the Senator that neither his party nor the Republican party will ever impede the march that this great country is about to make—the first in the world, I am glad to say—in adjusting to the demands of industry and commerce, that great instrument, money, the non-adjustment of which, as I have already stated, has, in my belief, caused more misery than was ever caused by war, pestilence, and famine.

But to resume at the point where I was interrupted:

The gold going out would tend constantly to restore the equilibrium between our prices and those of the gold-using countries, making the proportion of the gold outflow each year less than that of the year before. If there be included in this computation the remaining $100,000,000 of gold, which would remain after the outflow of the $600,000,000, we shall be compelled to come to the conclusion that the time when our stock of gold can be driven out will be almost indefinitely postponed.

But even should all our gold go by reason of the remonetization of silver, it will not be to the injury of the gold standard, but to its great advantage, and to the equally great advantage of the masses of the people, as well of this country, which the gold may leave, as of all countries to which it may go. It will make the "gold standard" consistent with the prosperity of the countries maintaining it. But instead of preserving the gold standard of to-day, which is a standard of wrong, it will inaugurate a gold standard that will approximate to a standard of justice.

The new "gold standard" that would be established by the outflow of our gold would be a standard of prices resulting from the influx into England, France, and Germany, the principal gold-using countries of Europe, of more than $600,000,000 of money.

So considerable an addition to their money-stock would raise prices in those countries, and by remaining there, would, with the current production, which we could spare to them, tend to maintain prices at a steady level. Such a condition would be an inestimable boon to the overburdened masses of Europe, and their prosperity would not be attained at the expense of the people of the United States. We could well afford to let gold go, since, by the coinage of silver, our own money volume would not be reduced. The rise of prices which it would effect in Europe would not only, as I have stated, secure better prices for our exported goods, but would undoubtedly enable us to maintain prices here at a substantial parity with those of Europe—that is to say, with those of the new, more rational and more beneficent gold standard which would be established by the full remonetization of silver in this country.

PRACTICALLY NO GOLD MONEY IN THE UNITED STATES.

But, aside altogether from this consideration, the gold that we already have is really a surplus—it is practically a dead and useless article. Gold, Mr. President, can not with entire truth be said at the present time to form any part of the money of this country. Who but a bank clerk ever sees a gold piece? With the exception of a few million dollars on the Pacific coast, gold is not really in cir-

JONES

culation in this country. It is performing no useful function whatsoever. While I am engaged in delivering these remarks I venture to say no Senator within the sound of my voice has in his pocket a single gold coin of any denomination whatever, or any paper representative of one.

This is the answer to the fear expressed by some Senators that when those who hold gold shall observe the enlargement of the money circulation by the issue of the proposed Treasury notes they will be likely to hoard it. They are already hoarding it. Every body knows that that is about all that gold is used for in this country. It is hardly possible for it to be hoarded to any greater extent than it is at the present time. So little is this metal in circulation that I do not deem it any exaggeration to say that there are millions of people in the United States, "native here, and to the manner born," who have never in all their lives seen a gold coin.

How absurd, then, is the claim that any loss is to be suffered by the alleged future hoarding of gold, or that any calamity can occur to 65,000,000 people by the disappearance of that which has long since disappeared.

THE ARGUMENT BASED ON OUR BALANCE OF TRADE.

One of the staple arguments of the advocates of the single gold standard is, that if our stock of gold were greatly reduced we should be unable to make payments to foreign countries in case the balance of trade turned against us. It is only through an excess of imports over exports that gold could go, and this country now produces of nearly all articles almost all that it consumes. With the exception of two years there has not been a balance of trade against us for fourteen years, as the following table will show:

Value of merchandise imported into, and exported from, the United States, from 1876 to 1889, inclusive; also annual excess of imports or of exports—specie values.

Year ending June 30—	Total exports.	Total imports.	Total exports and imports.	Excess of exports over imports.	Excess of imports over exports.
	Dollars.	Dollars.	Dollars.	Dollars.	Dollars.
1876	540, 384, 671	460, 741, 190	1, 001, 125, 861	79, 643, 481	....
1877	602, 475, 220	451, 323, 126	1, 053, 798, 346	151, 152, 094	....
1878	694, 865, 766	437, 051, 532	1, 131, 917, 298	257, 814, 234	....
1879	710, 439, 441	445, 777, 775	1, 156, 217, 216	264, 661, 666	....
1880	835, 638, 658	667, 954, 746	1, 503, 593, 404	167, 683, 912	....
1881	902, 377, 346	642, 664, 628	1, 545, 041, 974	259, 712, 718	....
1882	750, 542, 257	724, 639, 574	1, 475, 181, 831	25, 902, 683	....
1883	823, 639, 402	723, 180, 914	1, 547, 020, 316	100, 658, 488	....
1884	740, 513, 609	667, 697, 693	1, 408, 211, 302	72, 815, 916	....
1885	742, 189, 755	577, 527, 329	1, 319, 717, 084	161, 662, 426	....
1886	679, 524, 830	635, 436, 136	1, 314, 960, 966	44, 088, 694	....
1887	716, 183, 211	692, 319, 768	1, 408, 502, 977	23, 863, 443	....
1888	695, 954, 507	723, 957, 114	1, 419, 911, 621	....	28, 002, 607
1889	742, 401, 375	745, 131, 652	1, 487, 533, 027	....	2, 730, 277

This table shows that while for last year there was a balance against us of $2,730,277, and the year before of $28,002,607, for all former years from 1887 back to 1874 the balances were in our favor—all the way from $23,000,000 in 1887 to $265,000,000 in 1881. But the total want of significance so far as the movement of gold is concerned

JONES

attaching to any figures showing a balance of trade against the United States will be seen by an analysis of the figures for any one year. Let us take for example the imports and exports for 1889 and analyze them by countries.

I now present a table in which I place in one group the gold-using countries, and in another the silver and paper-using countries.

Exports and imports of the United States to and from the various gold-using and silver-using or paper-using countries of the world for the fiscal year ending June 30, 1889.

Countries.	Exports.	Imports.
Gold-using countries:		
Canada	$42,141,156	$43,009,473
Belgium	23,345,219	9,816,435
Denmark	3,003,937	846,904
France	46,120,041	69,566,618
Germany	68,602,594	81,742,546
Great Britain	382,981,674	178,269,067
Greece	165,079	983,923
Italy	12,604,848	17,992,149
Netherlands	15,062,989	10,950,843
Portugal and its possessions	3,266,814	1,282,550
Spain	11,946,348	4,636,661
Sweden and Norway	2,615,569	2,983,319
Turkey		4,667,731
British possessions in Africa	2,036,213	895,344
British possessions in Australia	12,321,980	5,998,211
Silver and paper using countries:		
Austria-Hungary	720,156	7,642,297
Russia	8,364,545	2,985,631
Mexico	11,486,896	21,253,601
Central America	4,325,923	8,414,019
Hawaii	3,375,661	12,847,740
Argentine Republic	9,293,856	5,454,618
Brazil	9,351,081	60,403,804
Chili	2,972,794	2,622,625
Peru	780,835	314,032
Colombia	3,821,017	4,263,519
Uruguay	2,102,848	2,986,964
Venezuela	3,738,961	10,392,569
Cuba	11,691,311	52,130,623
Hayti	5,340,270	5,211,704
Porto Rico	2,224,931	3,707,373
British West Indies	10,453,973	20,723,268
Dutch West Indies	887,778	654,320
China	6,477,512	18,508,678
India, British	4,330,413	20,029,601
India, Dutch	2,249,604	5,207,254
Japan	4,619,985	16,687,992

By this table it is seen that the only gold-using countries having a balance of trade against us are Canada, $868,317; France, $23,446,577; Greece, $823,824; Germany, $13,739,952; Italy, $5,387,301; Sweden and Norway, $367,850; Turkey, $4,687,731—making a total balance against us in gold-using countries, $49,321,452—against which we have a balance in our favor with Great Britain alone of over $200,000,000.

The balance against us in favor of all the silver using countries could of course be readily settled in silver; and by carefully noting the figures of the table last given it will be seen that it is in the last degree improbable that there will ever be a balance of trade against us in the gold using countries, taken as a whole.

Hence it is clear that if we had no gold at all we could readily settle all foreign balances that might be against us.

Nations, however, ultimately, and on the whole, square their accounts with commodities. Every nation must buy what it wants with its own products. In this country.especially have we nothing to fear, because any temporary balance against us could always be met by the yield from our own mines. No country has any difficulty by reason of any difference in money systems in buying what any other nation has to sell.

This view is supported by all writers on political economy. I need quote but one. Professor Cairnes, professor of political economy in the University College of London, in his able work on "Some unsettled questions in political economy" (1874), says:

It appears to me that the influence attributed by many able writers in the United States to the depreciation of the paper currency as regards its effects on the foreign trade of the country is, in a great degree, purely imaginary. An advance in the scale of prices, *measured in gold*, in a country, if not shared by other countries, will at once affect its foreign trade, giving an impulse to importations and checking the exportation of all commodities other than gold. A similar effect is very generally attributed by American writers to the action on prices of the greenback inconvertible currency.

But it may easily be shown that this is a complete illusion. Foreigners do not send their products to the United States to take back greenbacks in exchange. The return which they look for is either gold or the commodities of the country; and if these have risen in price in proportion as the paper money has been depreciated, how should the advance in paper prices constitute an inducement for them to send their goods thither? The nominal gain in greenbacks on the importation is exactly balanced by the nominal loss when those greenbacks came to be converted into gold or commodities. The gain may, in particular cases, exceed the loss, but, if it does, the loss will also, in other cases, exceed the gain. On the whole, and on an average, they can not but be the equivalents of each other.

Mr. President, the best place in the world where we can have gold is not in the Treasury of the United States, not in any sub-treasury, but in circulation, if not in our own country, then, in the foreign countries where our surplus products are sold. That is where gold would do us the most good by making money plentiful and prices correspondingly high. It does us no good here whatever, locked up as it always is, and doing none of the work of money, but simply reduces to the minimum the tax-paying and debt-paying power of our wheat- and cotton-growing communities.

An unjust money should not be tolerated, whatever the material of which it may be composed, and the people of this country will not tolerate it. They do not fear the outflow of gold. If, in order to retain it, they must continue to lose as they have been losing for the past fifteen years, they will favor its going, and raise a shout of joy when it does go. With a perfect money system in our own country the range of our domestic prices would continue stable and equitable without regard to the prices of foreign countries. Our foreign trade would take care of itself, and whatever the balances might be, they would be much oftener in our favor than against us, and in reality concern only the importing merchant and not the Government or the people of the United States. The difficulty of gold-using countries to get our money, in which to pay us the balances they would owe us, would be much greater than our difficulty in getting their money, in which to pay them the occasional balances we might owe them.

Much the more serious question, (if it be a serious question at all, which I deny) is how they shall get our money, not how we

JONES

shall get theirs. As the balances would be for the most part in our favor, it is for them to take such steps as may be necessary in order to pay us. But there is no just reason to apprehend difficulty in either case. A great country like the United States will have no trouble in buying the money of any other country at equitable rates—at rates regulated by the purchasing powers of the moneys of the two countries, respectively.

No country in the history of the world, having a money local to itself, has ever found the slightest difficulty in buying, upon ratios determined by the relative purchasing powers of the two kinds of money, a sufficient amount of foreign exchange (which simply means the money of another country) to meet all adverse balances of trade.

While earnestly advocating the full remonetization of silver and the maintenance in this country of a money volume sufficient to insure a steady level of prices and an unchanging value in the money unit, I entirely disclaim any desire for an inflation of the currency. My contention is that without silver we can not keep prices from further decline, and can not have enough money to serve the growing needs of population, industry, and commerce.

At the same time I can not refrain from expressing the conviction that, as between inflation and contraction, no careful student of history and of economic science can for a moment hesitate in deciding that the evils inflicted on society by contraction have been longer in duration and infinitely greater in degree than any that have ever resulted from inflation. During all periods in which there has been a generous increase in the money-volume of a country or of the world, activity and prosperity have been its accompaniment. I challenge the citation of an instance to the contrary.

With a volume of money increasing at a rate sufficient to meet the demands of a growing population, and especially if the money be such as will not leave the country, but, under all circumstances, will remain in it, to sustain prices, preserve equities, and reward labor, no country with a proper coördination of its industries can be otherwise than prosperous.

The property of mobility—of fluidity—which is so much lauded in gold, is precisely the property least to be desired in the money of a country, if that property of mobility or fluidity is to keep alternately bringing money into and taking it out of the country, disturbing prices and disarranging equities. When it comes, if it enters into circulation, prices rise ; when it goes, prices fall, and thus, instead of having a steady and level platform of prices on which the trade and industry of the Republic may rest, like the firm and level platform of liberty upon which all our citizens stand, we whose business it is to "see that the Republic take no harm," furnish our people with an "inclined plane" of finance on which all their business must be conducted. Men buying this month at the elevated end of the platform find themselves selling next month at the depressed end.

Whenever in the history of a country there has been least reliance on international money (gold) and more reliance on merely national money (even of paper when reasonable limits were placed upon its quantity), prosperity has been everywhere present. I need not recall to the minds of Senators the wave of prosperity that swept over this country when it was without any international money and resorted to the "greenback" currency.

When, as a result of the Franco-German war, France was deprived of international money, suspended specie payments, and resorted to a properly limited paper currency, her progress was unbounded.

JONES

No period in the history of Great Britain can compare for activity, prosperity, or achievement, with the twenty years preceding 1816, when specie payments were suspended, and during which period, as testified to by witnesses before the secret committee of Parliament, the discount rate of the Bank of England did not suffer a single change; whereas from that period to 1847 the rate was changed sixteen times, and from 1847 to 1874 as many as 274 times, the fluctuations being sometimes of the most violent character.

When gold threatens to leave Great Britain the rate of discount at the Bank of England is raised, with the view of discouraging, if not preventing, the outflow. Raising the rate of discount is like putting the brakes on a railroad train; lowering the rate is like letting off the brakes.

These changes were not due to any greater demand for money but to the movements of gold. There was frequently, in the condition of business, no warrant whatever for a rise in the rate of discount. The only reason for it was to prevent gold from performing what "our most conservative financiers" denominate its "noble" function of "mobility"—of "fluidity"—namely, the function of going "where it was wanted." This function of going "where it is wanted" is described as the great "mission" of gold, and it is assumed that it will never be wanted at more than one place at a time. Yet hear what the Chancellor of the exchequer of Great Britain said a few days ago in the House of Commons:

I admit that, as interested in the commerce and monetary system of this country, I feel a kind of shame that on the occasion of £2.000,000 or £3,000,000 of gold being taken from this country to Brazil, or any other country, it should immediately have the effect of causing a monetary alarm throughout the country. (Speech of the chancellor of the exchequer in the House of Commons, April 18, 1890.)

This is a suggestive admission, from so well-informed a source, as to the operation of the single gold standard. I commend it to those who would circumscribe and hamper the prosperity of this country by making gold alone the standard of all values.

I have thought it necessary, Mr. President, to state what I conceive to be the true principles of the science of money, the principles that, with the progress of time and growth of intelligence, must prevail the world over; because, without a clear understanding of the relation which the quantity of money in a country bears to the prosperity and happiness of its people, there would be no justification for an addition of either silver, gold, or any other form of money to the quantity already in circulation. If the value of money depends on quantity, then, as long as the world adheres to the automatic theory of money, my contention is that all the silver produced from all the mines of the world should be transmuted into coin; and even then, if the wants of the world continue to increase as they have been increasing, it is only a question of time, and that not far distant, when the combined supply of both metals will be insufficient to maintain the equities in time transactions.

The world having decreed to stand by the automatic system we are now dealing with the question as a practical one.

The only relief that can be had is to adhere strictly to that system, and give it full scope. Remove all legislative restrictions and let the world have the full benefit of all the precious metals that are yielded by the mines.

JONES

THE WORLD'S SUPPLY OF GOLD AND SILVER.

Since for thousands of years the world recognized both silver and gold as money, can anybody tell what has happened to render one of them unfitted for the money use?
No argument based on fluctuations in the current supplies of either of the metals can militate against the use of both as money. The fluctuation in the annual yield of both, taken together, is much less violent and less frequent than the fluctuation of either taken separately. By the use of both, society has much greater security against the evil of an insufficient money volume. While a large yield, now of one, and again of the other, has taken place, there is no instance in the history of the world of an extraordinary yield of both occurring simultaneously, except in the single instance of the first discovery of the mines of America. When the gold mines have been yielding largely, there has been no special increase of silver, and during the period when silver has been produced in comparatively large quantities the gold mines have been less productive.
This will be illustrated by the following table showing the yield of both gold and silver, from the discovery of America to the present time.

Annual average production of the precious metals throughout the world from the discovery of America to 1872.

[From Director of United States Mint.]

Periods.	Gold.	Silver.
1493-1520, average for each year	$3,855,000	$1,953,000
1521-1544......do	4,759,000	3,749,000
1545-1560......do	5,657,000	12,950,000
1561-1580......do	4,546,000	12,447,000
1581-1600......do	4,905,000	17,409,000
1601-1620......do	5,662,000	17,538,000
1621-1640 .....do	5,516,000	16,358,000
1641-1660......do	5,829,000	15,223,000
1661-1680......do	6,154,000	14,006,000
1681-1700......do	7,154,000	14,200,000
1701-1720, average for each year	8,520,000	14,779,000
1721-1740......do	12,681,000	17,921,000
1741-1760......do	16,356,000	22,158,000
1761-1780......do	13,761,000	27,128,000
1781-1800......do	11,823,000	36,534,000
1801-1810......do	11,815,000	37,161,000
1811-1820......do	7,606,000	22,474,000
1821-1830......do	9,448,000	19,141,000
1831-1840......do	13,484,000	24,788,000
1841-1850......do	36,393,000	32,434,000
1851-1855......do	131,268,000	36,827,000
1856-1860......do	136,946,060	37,611,000
1861-1865......do	131,728,000	45,764,000
1866-1870......do	127,537,000	55,652,000
1871-1872......do	113,431,000	81,849,000

JONES

World's production of gold and silver for the calendar years 1873 to 1889, inclusive.

Calendar years.	Gold.	Silver.		
	Value.	Fine ounces.	Market value.	Coining value.
1873...............	$96,200,000	63,267,000	$82,120,000	$81,800,000
1874...............	90,750,000	55,300,000	70,673,000	71,500,000
1875...............	97,500,000	62,262,000	77,578,000	80,500,000
1876...............	103,700,000	67,788,000	78,322,000	87,600,500
1877...............	114,000,000	62,648,000	75,240,000	81,000,000
1878...............	119,000,000	73,476,000	84,644,000	95,000,000
1879...............	109,000,000	74,250,000	83,383,000	96,000,000
1880...............	106,500,000	74,791,000	85,636,000	96,700,000
1881...............	103,000,000	78,890,000	89,777,000	102,000,000
1882...............	102,000,000	86,470,000	98,230,000	111,800,000
1883...............	95,400,000	89,177,000	96,986,000	115,800,000
1884...............	101,700,000	81,597,000	90,817,000	105,500,000
1885...............	108,400,000	91,652,000	97,564,000	118,500,000
1886...............	106,000,000	98,276,000	92,772,000	120,600,000
1887...............	105,300,000.	96,189,000	94,265,000	124,366,000
1888...............	109,900,000	109,911,000	103,316,000	142,107,000
1889...............	118,800,000	125,830,000	117,051,000	162,690,000

From this table it will be seen that from 1801 to 1820 the average yearly yield of gold was $9,710,500; of silver, $36,847,500—four of silver to one of gold.

From 1821 to 1840 the average yearly yield of gold was $11,466,000; of silver, $21,964,000—two of silver to one of gold.

From 1841 to 1860 the average yearly yield of gold was $85,150,000; of silver, $34,826,500—two and a half of gold to one of silver.

From 1861 to 1880 the yearly average yield of gold was $117,991,850; of silver, $68,043,900—nearly two of gold for one of silver.

From 1881 to 1889 the yearly average yield of gold was $105,500,000; of silver, $122,540,388—one-sixth more silver than gold.

From these figures it is plain that no continuous, extraordinary yield of silver, such as might warrant the slightest fear of an unnecessary addition to the money volume, is to be expected. On the other hand the continuous drain of gold for use in the arts, as dentistry, gold plate, jewelry, gilding, and articles of decoration generally, is, seriously encroaching upon the annual supply.

Both metals possess in common, and neither in any different degree from the other, all the qualities which are recognized as necessary in a commodity money. Silver enjoys in an equal degree with gold the quality of indestructibility, of divisibility, of malleability, and of resistance to chemical changes. The stock of both existing in the world (the product of all time) is estimated to be about equal, the production of the past 500 years being set down as—

Gold... $7,240,000,000
Silver... 7,435,000,000

That silver mining has not proved exceptionally profitable in this country is proved by the comparatively small number that have engaged in the business. This country has been thoroughly explored in the search for additional mines without any of great value being discovered. The allurements of the business lie in its uncertainty; and for the occasional prize that is drawn thousands of blanks are found. There is always enough hope of results to induce continued effort, but there is also sufficient doubt and discouragement to deter an undue number from engaging in the business.

The mines of Mexico have been worked for hundreds of years; and up to 1873 the business of silver mining in that country had all the stimulus that a parity at 15½ to 1 could give to it. It is not, therefore, probable that any material increase of output can be expected from that quarter.

Conceding, for the sake of the argument, the eventual possibility of so superabundant a yield of silver as to work injury and inequity to the interests of creditors, is it not manifest that it is in the power of society at all times to remedy the evil by a limitation of the coinage? And on the other hand, is it not equally manifest that for an insufficient supply there is no remedy?

If great mountains of silver should be discovered, does not Congress meet constantly? If there should seem to be too much, could not the coinage be readily limited to prevent depreciation? But, on the other hand, when we dedicate the monetary function solely to one metal, of which there is manifestly and admittedly the world over an insufficient supply, where is the remedy? What can Congress do to enlarge that supply? Absolutely nothing.

THE GOLD USED IN THE ARTS.

The Director of the United States Mint a few years ago estimated that of the $100,000,000 gold annually produced from the mines of the world $46,000,000 are consumed in the manufacture of jewelry, gold plate, plated ware, gold-leaf, etc., and in various processes of dentistry.

The single standard of gold, therefore, is maintained by the creditor nations in the face of the admitted fact that but $50,000,000 of that metal are annually added to the money stocks.

Not only is this encroachment of the commodity demand on the money supply becoming greater year by year, with the growth of population, but the supply of gold from the mines is itself becoming less, having declined from an average of $137,000,000 between 1856 and 1860 (the period of greatest yield from California and Australia), to an average of $107,000,000 for the past ten years. Of the entire gold supply of the world, nine-tenths of it have come from placer mines, readily discoverable and easily worked, because requiring little or no capital. All known fields of those are practically exhausted, and there is no reasonable prospect of the discovery of others. Hardy, adventurous, and skillful miners from the United States, and capitalists from all countries, have ransacked the world in vain for new fields of gold. Why, then, with the knowledge of those facts before us, should we discard from the full money use and function the only metal that gives to the world any prospect of relief from the money famine from which civilization is now suffering and from which, if silver be not speedily restored to its ancient use and function, the world is destined to suffer much more?

If it be conceivable that the demonetization of either metal were necessary, why demonetize that which promises the greater and more steady yield? If for any reason society should decide that one of the metals should be discarded, should it not rather be that one which promises the smaller future yield, than that which promises the larger?

Silver is the money-metal best suited to the mass of the people, and to the variety and character of transactions that constitute the interchanges of daily life. The supplies of both metals if united by

JONES

law, in the full money function, would have a steadiness of value which can not be attained by either separately.

TREASURY NOTES SHOULD NOT BE REDEEMED IN BULLION.

The proposition to redeem the proposed treasury notes in silver bullion or in anything but lawful money of the United States will never meet the approval of the people. What the people of this country want is money, and what they should have is money. These notes will represent full value received, the evidence of which is the bullion in possession of the Government. When issued, they will enter into circulation. They will have to do the work of money among the people. They will go to make up the volume of the currency. On the basis of that volume each dollar acquires a certain value, and represents a given amount of sacrifice. On that volume, and on those conditions, bargains will be made, prices established, debts contracted, values adjusted, and equities created. If any portion of that money be withdrawn from circulation (for that is what "redemption" means) without an equivalent amount of money in some other form being issued to take its place, the circulation will to that extent be contracted, every dollar in circulation will increase in value, prices will fall, property-values established on the basis of the larger circulation will shrink, and equities will be destroyed.

The redemption of any number of those notes in silver bullion means the withdrawal of so many dollars of money from circulation and the destruction of so much of the money of the country. Money is not a thing that can be destroyed with impunity. It should be kept in use among the people. It is to industry what the blood is to the human body; it is the life-giving and life-sustaining medium. The money volume of a country should not be subject to frequent and violent changes. In a new and growing country, it should be characterized by that steady accretion that characterizes the increase in the quantity of blood in the human body as it progresses from infancy to maturity. It is no more unreasoning, empirical, or unscientific to be alternately withdrawing blood from, and injecting blood into, a human body than to be constantly contracting and expanding the money volume of the country. And as activity of circulation of the blood is essential to the health of the body, so activity of circulation in money is indispensable to the well-being of society. The possession of no mere commodity, whatever its value, will compensate a country for the destruction of any considerable portion of its money, upon the entire volume of which vast equities rest.

MONEY SHOULD BE REDEEMABLE IN ALL THINGS.

Money should be redeemed in all things; not in one thing alone. The peculiar characteristic of true money, that which distinguishes it from all other things whatsoever and constitutes it a prime factor in civilization, is that it is at all times redeemable in any thing that is on sale. Being an order for property, it should be redeemed in any form of disposable property which the holder may desire.

A guinea—

said Adam Smith—

may be considered as a bill for a certain quantity of necessaries and conveniences upon all the tradesmen in the neighborhood.

Any form of money, the condition of whose existence depends on redeemability in one thing alone, can not be money in the full sense,

JONES

and whenever an urgent demand for real money springs up the other ceases altogether to be money.

The redemption of money should be reciprocal between the Government and the people and between and among all individuals in the community. It should not only be redeemable by the Government by acceptance for taxes but also redeemable by and among the people for all property for sale and services for hire. Its quantity should be so regulated as that its unit (the dollar) should neither increase nor diminish in value, and it should be kept constantly in circulation, and not be permitted to lie uselessly in the Treasury. Any other money than this is to a certain extent counterfeit; it is false money, because when most needed it fails to be money and has to be "redeemed" in something else (gold) which can not be got except at ruinous sacrifice.

It is of the very essence of money—its pith and marrow and protoplasm—that it should be a legal tender, a universal solvent, the ultimate of payment, and redeemable, at the prices ruling, in everything that is on sale. If the volume of such money be properly regulated, while there may from time to time be variations in the prices of particular articles, the general range of prices will be maintained practically undisturbed.

What an absurdity it is for the Government to put its stamp on one thing in order to make it redeemable in another thing imprinted with the same stamp, but which nobody wants except for the purpose of getting a third thing that could have been got just as well without the intervention of the second. As well might he who, wanting water, is given a silver cup wherewith to get it, but on going to the spring is forbidden to drink until he exchanges his silver cup for a gold one.

The real reason why it is insisted that all other things than gold shall be exchangeable into gold is that gold is getting dearer by reason of decreasing supply and increasing populations. The necessity for convertibility into gold implies that, in ordinary times, a range of prices higher than the gold range will prevail, and when, by reason perhaps of increased activity of business, redemption comes to be demanded prices are at once precipitated to those of the gold standard and below, to the great advantage of the creditor classes, who, as owners of bonds, may be considered in the language of the stock exchange "long" on money, and to the equally great injury of the producing class, who, being in debt, may be considered as having sold money "short."

The supreme consideration is that the money of a country shall be so regulated as that prices may not fall from any cause inhering in the money system. The value of money—in other words, the sacrifice necessary to obtain it—should be no greater at one time than at another. In order to effect that object of prime consequence, to maintain the value of money unchanging, there should be no hesitancy whatever in changing the material of which it is made.

Nobody who has reflected on the subject for a moment doubts that what gave "value" or exchangeable power to the greenback was not the promise made on its face, without date, to pay a dollar, but the inscription on its back which declared it a legal tender for all dues and demands, public and private, except duties on imports. It was a misfortune to mankind that the words "promise to pay" were printed on it, because by it millions were led to believe that the "value" or exchangeable power resided in the promise instead of in the legal-tender power conferred upon it.

JONES

There is no object in redeeming in gold, except to maintain gold prices, that is to say, the range of prices prevailing in gold-using countries, and as those prices are constantly trending downward, any country that insists on maintaining the gold standard must accept the consequences in a corresponding fall of prices. The advocates of the gold standard, in effect, maintain that no matter to what extreme prices may fall, we must bo content—we must bow in humble submission to the inevitable, since, in their view, it is more necessary to maintain the sacredness of the gold standard than to establish justice, promote prosperity, or to maintain equity in all time transactions.

It is in no way necessary, on account of any intrinsic or inherent quality of gold, that we should have that particular metal, and that alone, for money.

It is boasted that gold is a universal measure. Why is it universal? Why is gold accepted in every country of the world? Not because the gold is wanted for any quality inherent in the metal, but because it is an order for property in gold-using countries, such as England, France, and Germany, whose trade is largely a foreign trade. At whatever rate gold will exchange in England, it will exchange in all countries having trade relations with England, because it is an order for goods in a country with which they are dealing. Will not the money of this country equally, and for like reasons, whether gold or silver, have acceptability in every country with which the United States have trade relations? Not for any quality inherent in the metal, but because it is an order for property in the United States. Will it not be willingly accepted by those who wish to buy in this country?

POSSIBLE EFFECT OF REDEMPTION IN BULLION.

In order to see the effect of the redemption of these Treasury notes in bullion, we have but to look at the possibilities of the situation. Suppose there were in the Treasury $300,000,000 worth of that bullion, which, by the taking up, little by little, and month by month, of the amount not used in the arts, would be taken by the Treasury at or about par. Then, suppose that for any reason, such as fear of approaching panic or otherwise, $100,000,000 of the Treasury notes were suddenly presented for redemption, and canceled, and the bullion as suddenly put on the market, what would it be worth? What would gold bullion be worth if it had not the privilege of coinage, and if $100,000,000 of it, deprived of the money use, was suddenly put on the market? Can there be a doubt that the abrupt output of so large a quantity would have the effect of immediately and enormously depreciating its value? In the case under consideration, the result would be that the silver remaining in the Treasury would not bring one-fourth the sum necessary to redeem the outstanding Treasury notes, so that not only would a heavy loss result to the Government, but, by reason of the sudden and serious contraction of the money volume, an infinitely greater loss would result to all the people.

But if it be deemed a remote contingency that any extraordinary amount would in that manner be suddenly taken from the Treasury, there is another danger which can not be put aside as improbable, but which, on the contrary, is to be looked for with almost absolute certainty, and to my mind, constitutes an irremovable and insurmountable objection to any system of bullion redemption.

A large number of merchants in London need, monthly, millions of dollars worth of silver to make payments in India. They will naturally want to get it at the lowest price, and it is not to their advantage to intensify the competition for it. On the contrary, it is to their direct advantage to depress the price to the lowest possible point.

As the Treasury of the United States would buy silver at the lowest price, the London merchants would refuse to enter the open market in competition with our Government for its purchase. But no sooner could the silver be stored in the vaults of the Treasury, than the agents of the London merchants would appear, and before any opportunity had offered for a favorable change in the price of the bullion, could present as many millions of these notes as might suit their purpose, and receive bullion therefor. A Secretary of the Treasury who conscientiously believed that it was his duty to maintain the gold standard at all hazards, would naturally feel compelled—certainly it would be in his power—to put out whatever amount of bullion he might deem necessary to accomplish that purpose, even if it all had to go.

Thus the United States Treasury would become the convenient and capacious conduit through which silver should immediately flow from this country to England, depriving our people, notwithstanding the legislative measures for their relief, of practically all use of silver as money, inasmuch as the four and a half-million dollars of Treasury notes would be withdrawn and canceled about as soon as issued.

Thus would our Treasury Department be made practically the purchasing agent in this country of any syndicate or combination of English merchants who might desire silver for the East India trade.

If it be said that no Secretary of the Treasury would attempt thus to defeat the will of the people as expressed in the law, the sufficient reply is that a conscientious man who believes that the honor of the United States is pledged to the maintenance of the gold standard, and that it is indispensable to the prosperity of the people, will exercise all the power vested in him by law to prevent a departure from that standard, and will regard himself as for the time being the savior of the Republic by keeping it from "the edge of so dangerous a peril" as the execution of the people's will.

Certainly no man will deny to the present Secretary of the Treasury entire rectitude of motive in all his conduct. From the well-known fact that since the passage of the limited coinage act of 1878 all our Secretaries have refrained from purchasing more silver than they were compelled to do by the mandatory provision of that law, it is reasonable to infer that none of them, if called upon to execute a law containing a silver bullion redemption clause, such as is suggested, would feel called upon to make a net purchase of more than $2,000,000 worth in each month; and that none of them would hesitate to exchange for Treasury notes all the monthly purchases of bullion in excess of that amount.

A PLANK FROM THE REPUBLICAN PLATFORM.

I must be pardoned for directing the attention of Senators on this side of the Chamber to a short declaration of the last Republican National Convention:

The Republican party is in favor of the use of both gold and silver as money.

If party platforms mean anything that clause meant that the Republican party went before the country pledged to the use and to the equal and non-discriminating use of both silver and gold as money. It was well known that throughout the entire West the question

JONES

of the remonetization of silver was deemed of vital importance, and party orators and the party press, throughout that entire section were severe in their denunciation of the prior administration of its unfriendly attitude toward silver.

I wish in all solicitude and sincerity to advise my Republican friends of the East that this plank in the party platform was construed by the Republicans of the West to mean precisely what it says. They are looking with confidence to this Congress for such action as will fittingly embody in the statutes the principle laid down by the party now in the responsible direction of the Government.

SHALL WE BE FLOODED WITH SILVER?

We are told that if silver is given free access to the mints we shall be flooded with it from all parts of the world. Does anybody show where the flood of silver is to come from? Where are the reservoirs that contain it? Not in England, where it is difficult for the people even to get a sufficiency of it for small change to transact the business of the country: not in Germany, where the scarcity of money was so pressing that the government had to abandon the idea of selling silver. Though the stock in France is large her people will never give it up. Silver has been the "shield and buckler" of the French Republic. All she has is coined at the ratio of $15\frac{1}{2}$ ounces of silver to 1 of gold, and its shipment to this country would involve a loss to France, not only of the 3 per cent. difference between the French relation ($15\frac{1}{2}$ to 1) and ours (which is 16 to 1), but of 3 per cent. additional in the cost of gathering and shipping it. And after that could only exchange them for Treasury notes. The silver stock in India and the Orient is performing indispensable duty as money, and no "flood" of it can be expected from that quarter. From time immemorial India has been absorbing all the surplus silver of the world. She has never got so much as to appease her appetite for more. So insatiable is her desire for that metal that she has long been known as the "Sink of Silver." China has not a piece of the metal that she can dispose of. Mexico has no stock whatever of silver on hand, except the limited number of coined pieces forming her moderate money circulation, and not a dollar of it can be spared. No country of Central or South America has any surplus silver. Every piece of coined silver in every country in the world is part of the monetary circulation of that country, and even when of short weight and classified as a mere "token" is passing at par as full valued money. No gain could possibly accrue, therefore, to the owners of coined silver anywhere by shipping it to this country for any purpose, and there is no surplus stock of bullion anywhere.

If anybody doubts this statement let him make the attempt in all the money centers of the world to buy from accumulated stock even $5,000,000 worth of it. He will fail to get it in London, Paris, Berlin, Calcutta, New York, or San Francisco, or in all combined. There is no source from which to get silver except the current supply from the mines, and whatever that is now it is not likely ever greatly to increase. The occupation of mining is not attractive to many, and in the nature of the case the number who follow it will always be comparatively few. The Argonauts of old were but a small band of hardy adventurers; those of the new era are destined to bear no larger proportion to the population. But even were this not so, nature herself draws the line. To the eye of the experienced prospector silver mines are as discernible on the surface of the earth as are mountains, and the world has been explored in vain for further "finds." Those who talk, therefore, of "floods" of silver coming

JONES

here for coinage simply show their ignorance of existing conditions.
I may add that of all the shafts that have been sunk for silver
mines in the world where they have found silver croppings on top
in ninety-nine out of every hundred, and I think I am stating it
moderately, the veins have not penetrated the earth, mineralized,
fertilized, to the depth of 50 feet, rarely have they penetrated the earth
to a depth exceeding 1,200 feet, and the most prolific yield of silver
mines has been from a depth not exceeding 800 feet.

The very fact, Mr. President, that, with all the world searching
for gold and silver mines—a search that has continued throughout
all history—the amount of the two metals yielded by the mines is
about equal, shows that the historical relation existing between them
is the relation at which they can be profitably produced.

It is apparent that if there were a great advantage in the production of silver over gold, at the relation of 15¼ to 1, that advantage
would be seen in the largely preponderant production of silver;
but instead we find that the result of thousands of years of mining
has given us about equal quantities of both metals.

CAN THE UNITED STATES ALONE HOLD THE METALS AT A PARITY ?

We are told that the United States, unaided, can not, if it would,
restore silver to a parity with gold—that no one nation acting alone
can achieve so difficult a feat. But it is incapable of denial that
throughout all vicissitudes of production of gold and silver from
1803 to 1873 the law of France—one nation alone—accomplished it.

As I have shown in greater detail elsewhere, by reference to the
table of annual production of the metals, it will be observed that
from 1803 to 1820, the production was in the proportion of four dollars of silver to one of gold; from 1821 to 1840 two of silver to one
of gold, from 1841 to 1850 one dollar of silver, to one of gold, from 1851
to 1860 four dollars of gold to one of silver, from 1861 to 1865 three
of gold to one of silver, from 1866 to 1870 two of gold to one of silver,
in 1871 and 1872 one-and-a-half of gold to one of silver. Notwithstanding these extreme variations in the relative annual production
the law of France constituted a ligature sufficient to hold the metals
in line at the ratio of 15¼ to 1, and this not for France alone but
for the whole world. If that period does not offer sufficient proof of
the power of law, under varying conditions of supply, to tie the
metals together and keep them so, no degree of proof will suffice,
for the vacillations of their relative production have been greater
during this century than at any former period in the history of the
world.

IS AN INTERNATIONAL AGREEMENT NECESSARY ?

If that could be done by a nation with a population of 25,000,000
to 35,000,000, what difficulty could be experienced by a nation of
65,000,000 in accomplishing the same result ? Yet we are told that
international agreement is necessary to restore silver to its ancient
right as a full-money metal. Those who suggest such an agreement
forget that while this nation is a borrower of money, the first and
principal nation to demonetize silver is the greatest money lender
known to history. Is it for a moment to be supposed that the shrewd
English creditor classes will enter into any agreement which will
deprive them of the spoils of so delicate and ingenious a system
of usury, a system not only not banned by law, but, on the contrary,
having the special approval and protection of statutes, and the active
support and approval of all the complaisant moralists, philosophers,
and financiers of the age ?

JONES

While they are dilligently gathering in the proceeds of this operation a diversion is kept up for the occupation and amusement of dilettant financiers and economists, by invoking a discussion of the ratio that should be maintained between the metals. The ratio is the pretext on which conference after conference has been called.

The advocates of the single gold standard contend that hostile legislation had no influence in effecting the separation of the metals, and that the reversal of that legislation can not and will not restore them to a parity unless the principal commercial nations of the western world join in the work of rehabilitation. As illustrating the force of law on the relation of the metals I will read a suggestive paragraph from the report of the Royal Commission of England (1886), Part I, section 192:

> Now, undoubtedly, the date which forms the dividing line between an epoch of approximate fixity in the relative value of gold and silver, and one of marked instability, is the year when the bimetallic system which had previously been in force in the Latin Union ceased to be in full operation, and we are irresistibly led to the conclusion that the operation of that system, established as it was in countries the population and commerce of which w ere considerable, exerted a material influence upon the relative value of the two metals.
>
> So long as that system was in force we think that, notwithstanding the changes in the production and use of the precious metals, it kept the market price of silver approximately steady at the ratio fixed by law between them, namely, 15½ to 1. Nor does it appear to us *a priori* unreasonable to suppose that the existence in the Latin Union of a bimetallic system with a ratio of 15½ to 1 fixed between the two metals should have been capable of keeping the market price of silver steady at approximately that ratio.

The paragraph quoted ascribes the effect thus produced to the bimetallic treaty of the Latin Union, a combination of Italy, Belgium, Switzerland, and France, entered into in 1865 for the purpose of maintaining similar conditions of coinage. But it will be observed that, so far as the ratio was concerned, precisely the same effect had been produced by France alone during the sixty-two years from the passage of its law of 1803 to 1865.

Not only did the French law keep the metals together at a time when the larger annual yield was of silver, but it kept them together when the larger annual yield was of gold. Had not that law been in operation during the '50's, when a flood of gold poured from the mines of California and Australia, gold would have fallen, as in early times it more than once fell, to the ratio of 1 to 10, at which but 10 ounces of silver (instead of 15½) would buy an ounce of gold. Thus the law of one country alone, a country then of not one-half the present population of the United States, held the metals together, so that to whatever extent gold fell in relation to commodities from 1848 to 1865, by reason of the large output of the mines, silver fell to the same extent, notwithstanding the enormous decrease in its production relatively to gold during that period.

What is claimed for law in this connection is not that it directly controls the relative values of gold and silver any more than of anything else, but that on the slightest separation of the metals there instantly arises, under the law of the double standard, a demand for the cheaper metal, while the demand for the dearer one is suspended. In this way the double standard accommodates itself to the law of supply and demand, which is admitted to be the governing factor in the determination of value. It is not contended that a small or insignificant country could keep the metals together, but all experience goes to show that a great nation like the United States would have no difficulty whatever in doing so.

So thoroughly are the advantages of the gold standard to the creditor classes recognized in England that the English Commissioners, who, for form's sake, have been sent to the several monetary conferences held on the continent, have never been invested by their Government with any power whatever. And it is but a few weeks since the House of Commons overwhelmingly voted down a proposition made in good faith by Mr. Samuel Smith, looking to the calling of a new conference, which was supported by petitions to Parliament signed by 60,000 persons not merely as individuals, but as representing large organizations of the toilers of England.

The ratio is not the difficulty. Those who wanted silver demonetized do not want it added to the money volume of the world at any ratio. Why then shall we wait? Macauley, commenting on the impregnability of intrenched prerogative, observed that if the announcement of the discovery of the law of gravitation had militated against the personal interests of any vested or privileged class, its general acceptance might have been long postponed. Shall we, then, postpone relief to the suffering industries of this country till we can secure from the privileged classes, from the money-lenders of the world, an agreement to cease their exactions?

No, Mr. President, we need not wait, and we *will* not wait. All that is necessary is to *act*, and so far as the rules of order and of parliamentary procedure will permit, we propose to act, promptly and decisively. The world can not expect the initiatory movement for any change to be taken by those whose interests are served by the continuance of present conditions. Such conditions being consistent with their own welfare, they find no difficulty in arriving at the conclusion that they are for the welfare of society at large.

The dogma that cupidity is a synonym for virtue will never fail to find ready converts among the beneficiaries.

* * * Plate sin with gold,
And the strong lance of Justice hurtless breaks.

CONCLUSION.

I predict that the restoration of silver to its birthright, Mr. President, will mark an epoch in the history of this country. It will place in circulation an amount of money commensurate with our increasing population. It will give assurance to our languishing industries that the volume of our circulating medium is not to continue shrinking, and that the tendency of prices shall no longer be downward. It will increase the wages of labor and the prices of the products of labor; it will reduce the price of bonds and other forms of money futures, it will lighten, but not inequitably, the burden of mortgages; it will increase largely, though not unjustly, the debt-paying and tax-paying power of the people. It will loosen the grasp of the creditor from the throat of the debtor.

By the remonetization of silver, money will cease to be the object of commerce, and will again become its beneficent instrument. Activity will replace stagnation, movement will supplant inertia, courage will banish fear; confidence will dispel doubt; hope will supersede despair.

The lifting up of silver to its rightful plane by the side of gold will set in motion all the latent energies of the people. It will banish involuntary idleness, by putting every willing man to work. It will revive business, and reanimate the heart and hope of the masses. Capital, no longer fearing a fall in prices, will turn into productive avenues. The hoards of money lying idle in the bank vaults will come out to bless and enrich alike their owners and the community

JONES

at large; while the millions of dollars now invested at low interest in gilt-edged securities will seek more profitable investment in the busy field of industry, where they will be utilized in the payment of wages and the consequent dissemination of comfort and happiness among the people.

And this it will accomplish not for the United States alone, but for civilization. For it is not too much to say, Mr. President, that upon the decision of this question depend consequences more momentous than upon that of any other question of public policy within the memory of this generation. In a broader sense than any other question attracting the general attention of mankind it is a question of civilization. It embodies the hopes and aspirations of our race.

The act of Congress which shall happily solve it will constitute a decree of emancipation as veritable as any that ever freed serf from thraldom, but more universal in its application. It will proclaim the freedom of the white race the world over, it will lift the bowed head of labor, it will hush the threnody of toil. It will inaugurate the true renaissance—a renaissance of *prosperity*, without which industry, learning, science, literature, art, are but as apples of Sodom. (Applause in the galleries.)

JONES

INDEX.

JONES

JONES

www.ingramcontent.com/pod-product-compliance
Lightning Source LLC
Chambersburg PA
CBHW030630270326
41927CB00007B/1380